D1084185

NEW BEARINGS
IN ENGLISH POETRY

By the same Author

FOR CONTINUITY

THE COMMON PURSUIT

REVALUATION

MILL ON BENTHAM AND COLERIDGE

EDUCATION AND THE UNIVERSITY

D. H. LAWRENCE: NOVELIST

THE GREAT TRADITION

'ANNA KARENINA' AND OTHER ESSAYS

ENGLISH LITERATURE IN OUR TIME
AND THE UNIVERSITY

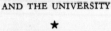

With Denys Thompson

CULTURE AND ENVIRONMENT

With Michael Yudkin

TWO CULTURES?
THE SIGNIFICANCE OF C. P. SNOW

Edited by the same Author

DETERMINATIONS

With Q. D. Leavis

LECTURES IN AMERICA

DICKENS THE NOVELIST

NEW BEARINGS IN ENGLISH POETRY

A STUDY OF
THE CONTEMPORARY SITUATION

F. R. Leavis

NEW EDITION

1971
CHATTO & WINDUS
LONDON

PUBLISHED BY

Chatto and Windus Ltd.

LONDON

★

Clarke, Irwin & Co. Ltd.

TORONTO

ISBN 0 7011 0893 2

FIRST PUBLISHED 1932
REPRINTED 1937, 1942
NEW EDITION 1950
REPRINTED 1954
REPRINTED 1959
REPRINTED 1961
REPRINTED 1971

Reproduced and Printed in Great Britain by
Redwood Press Limited
Trowbridge & London

Contents

To

H.L. and Q.D.L.

Nightingales, Anangke, a sunset or the meanest flower
Were formerly the potentialities of poetry,
But now what have they to do with one another
With Dionysus or with me?

   *   *   *   *   *

Microscopic anatomy of ephemerides,
Power-house stacks, girder-ribs, provide a crude base ;
But man is what he eats, and they are not bred
Flesh of our flesh, being unrelated
Experientially, fused in no emotive furnace.

            RONALD BOTTRALL

  What we cannot understand, it is very common, and
indeed a very natural thing, for us to undervalue ; and it
may be suspected that some of the merriest witticisms
which have been uttered against Mr Wordsworth, have
had their origin in the pettishness and dissatisfaction of
minds, unaccustomed and unwilling to make, either to
others or to themselves, any confession of incapacity.

          J. G. LOCKHART

Prefatory Note

THIS book, as the title indicates, does not offer itself as a survey of the verse—even the good verse—produced in our time. It starts from certain general considerations about poetry and, in particular, the relation of poetry to the modern world. How little I suppose these considerations to be original the book will make plain : it is largely an acknowledgment, vicarious as well as personal, of indebtedness to a certain critic and poet. Indeed they have been commonplaces for some years. They may be found habitually referred to and employed as such in *The Calendar*, that uniquely intelligent review which, from 1925 to 1927, was, it is hardly excessive to say, the critical consciousness of the younger adult generations. And yet it was not because they were commonplaces that *The Calendar*, for all its brilliance, was condemned to die of neglect.

If I am embarrassed at all, it is at seeing the simple—perhaps even naïve—way in which I have put them. I have deliberately put them in the simplest terms, believing that so they are most irresistible : for if they are commonplaces they have not, I have ample grounds for contending, been as common in effective acceptance as they should have been.

In any case, my main concern is with the concrete : to discuss critically what seems to me most significant in contemporary poetry, ' significance ' being defined by the generalities that I venture upon. I have endeavoured to confine myself as strictly as possible to literary criticism, and to remember that poetry is made of words. Many interesting and apparently relevant questions concerning the present and future of poetry that have presented themselves, and that the reader may expect to find dealt with, I have therefore dismissed, hoping by this asceticism to ensure a cleaner impact.

The reader, missing also certain poets whom he expected to find, may complain that my criterion of significance is too rigorous. To this I can only reply that I meant it to be rigorous : nevertheless, I do not think that I have left out much work that is important by any serious standards. There may, of course, especially in America, be important poets of whom I am ignorant : I hope that American readers will be placated by observing that two out of my three main subjects are Americans by birth.

There are certain serious and intelligent verse-writers whom (though I respect them) I have not dealt with because they seem to me not poets. I preferred to pass them by rather than introduce them only for critical dismissal. The necessary criticism upon them, it seems to me, makes itself if my valuations of Mr Eliot, Mr Pound and Hopkins are accepted. I notice that in any case the necessities of compression have led sometimes (especially in the second chapter) to effects that might be found ironical.

I

Poetry and the Modern World

POETRY matters little to the modern world. That is, very little of contemporary intelligence concerns itself with poetry. It is true that a very great deal of verse has come from the press in the last twenty years, and the uninterested might take this as proving the existence both of a great deal of interest in poetry and of a great deal of talent. Indeed, anthologists do. They make, modestly, the most extravagant claims on behalf of the age. 'It is of no use asking a poetical renascence to conform to type,' writes Mr J. C. Squire in his *Prefatory Note* to *Selections from Modern Poets*. 'There are marked differences in the features of all those English poetical movements which have chiefly contributed to the body of our "immortal" poetry.... Should our literary age be remembered by posterity solely as an age during which fifty men had written lyrics of some durability for their truth and beauty, it would not be remembered with contempt. It is in that conviction that I have compiled this anthology.' Mr Harold Monro, introducing *Twentieth Century Poetry*, is more modest and more extravagant:

' Is it a great big period, or a minutely small?
Reply who can! Somebody with whom I was
talking said: " They are all of them only poetical
persons—*not* poets. Who will be reading them a
century hence?" To which I answered: " There
are so many of them that, a century hence, they
may appear a kind of Composite Poet; there may
be 500 excellent poems proceeding from 100
poets mostly not so very great, but well worth
remembering a century hence." '

Such claims are symptoms of the very weakness
that they deny: they could have been made only
in an age in which there were no serious standards
current, no live tradition of poetry, and no public
capable of informed and serious interest. No one
could be seriously interested in the great bulk of
the verse that is culled and offered to us as the fine
flower of modern poetry. For the most part it is
not so much bad as dead—it was never alive.
The words that lie there arranged on the page
have no roots: the writer himself can never have
been more than superficially interested in them.
Even such genuine poetry as the anthologies of
modern verse do contain is apt, by its kind and
quality, to suggest that the present age does not
favour the growth of poets. A study of the latter
end of *The Oxford Book of Victorian Verse* leads to
the conclusion that something has been wrong
for forty or fifty years at the least.

For it seems unlikely that the number of potential poets born varies as much from age to age as literary history might lead one to suppose. What varies is the use made of talent. And the use each age makes of its crop of talent is determined largely by the preconceptions of ' the poetical ' that are current, and the corresponding habits, conventions and techniques. There are, of course, other very important conditions, social, economic, philosophical and so on ; but my province is that of literary criticism, and I am confining myself as far as possible to those conditions which it rests with the poet and the critic to modify—those which are their immediate concern.

Every age, then, has its preconceptions and assumptions regarding poetry : these are the essentially poetical subjects, these the poetical materials, these the poetical modes. The most influential are apt to be those of which we are least aware. The preconceptions coming down to us from the last century were established in the period of the great Romantics, Wordsworth, Coleridge, Byron, Shelley and Keats. To attempt to define them is to risk misrepresenting them, for it is largely in their being vague and undefined that their power has lain. Their earliest formulation is to be found, perhaps, in the *Dedication* (dated 1756) of Joseph Warton's *Essay on the Genius and Writings of Pope*. What Warton, con-

sciously challenging the prevailing ideas, puts
explicitly, afterwards came to be implicitly
assumed.

> We do not, it should seem, sufficiently attend to
> the difference there is between a MAN OF WIT, a MAN
> OF SENSE, and a TRUE POET.   Donne and Swift were
> undoubtedly men of wit, and men of sense : but
> what traces have they left of PURE POETRY ?

The question would seem to determine the
spirit of the affirmation : any doubt that may
remain, both affirmation and question in the
following combine to settle :

> The sublime and the pathetic are the two chief
> nerves of all genuine poesy.   What is there trans-
> cendently sublime or pathetic in Pope ?

Warton goes on to classify the English Poets :

> In the first class I would place our only three
> sublime and pathetic poets ; SPENSER, SHAKESPEARE,
> MILTON.

The collocation is decisive : it defines with
sufficient precision the nineteenth-century idea of
the poetical. Donne, we may note, Warton
places in the third class. The reign of the idea is
challenged when Donne comes to be associated
with Shakespeare in contrast to Spenser and
Milton. How universal and unquestioned it had
become in the Victorian Age Matthew Arnold
may be cited to prove. His evidence is the more

significant in that it was unwitting, for he regarded himself as a critic of the ideas about poetry
current in his day.

> Though they may write in verse, though they may
> in a certain sense be masters of the art of versifica-
> tion, Dryden and Pope are not classics of our
> poetry, they are classics of our prose.[1]

> The difference between genuine poetry and the
> poetry of Dryden, Pope, and all their school, is
> briefly this : their poetry is conceived and composed
> in their wits, genuine poetry is conceived and com-
> posed in the soul.[2]

—Arnold, that is, shares with his age a prejudice
against recognizing as poetry anything that is not,
in the obvious sense of Milton's formula, ' simple,
sensuous, and passionate.' Poetry, it was assumed,
must be the direct expression of simple emotions,
and these of a limited class : the tender, the
exalted, the poignant, and, in general, the sympathetic. (It is still quite common to come to the
University from school doubting whether satire
can be poetry.) Wit, play of intellect, stress of
cerebral muscle had no place : they could only
hinder the reader's being ' moved '—the correct
poetical response.[3]

[1] *Essays in Criticism.*   Second Series : *The Study of Poetry.*
[2] *Ibid.*, *Thomas Gray.*
[3] ' Poetry tells you about things that have happened long ago, and
it tells you about them in language that is rich with an antique idiom.
. . . The poet must, I think, be regarded as striving after the simplicity
of a childish utterance.   His goal is to think as a child, to understand

There is something further to be noted of 'the poetical' in the nineteenth century. It comes out if one considers these half-a-dozen well-known and representative poems : *La Belle Dame Sans Merci, Mariana, The Lady of Shalott, The Blessed Damozel*, Morris's *The Nymph's Song to Hylas, A Forsaken Garden*, O'Shaughnessy's *Ode*. Nineteenth-century poetry, we realize, was characteristically preoccupied with the creation of a dream-world.[1] Not all of the poetry, or all of the poets : but the preoccupation was characteristic. So that when a poetaster like O'Shaughnessy, with nothing personal to communicate, was moved by the desire to write poetry he produced this :

> We are the music-makers,
>   And we are the dreamers of dreams,
> Wandering by lone sea-breakers,
>   And sitting by desolate streams ;
> World-losers and world forsakers,
>   On whom the pale moon gleams. . . .

The preoccupation, the habit, then, became a dominant element in the set of ideas, attitudes and sentiments constituting 'the poetical' for the nineteenth century, and may often be seen to be present and potent when it is not avowed or even wittingly entertained. Consider, for instance,

as a child. He must deliver himself—and the poetic task is the same in every age—from the burden of the intellect of his day and the complexity of the forms of speech which it involves.'—J. M. Thorburn, *Art and the Unconscious*, p. 70.

[1] Mr Eliot has pointed this out in *Homage to John Dryden*.

Andrew Lang's sonnet, *The Odyssey*. Lang (born in 1844) was a scholar and a man of taste, with a feeling for language and a desire to write poetry —with, in short, all the qualifications of a poet except the essential one, the need to communicate something of his own. His sonnet is one of the most interesting of the many documents of like value that are to be found in *The Oxford Book of English Verse*. It illustrates very neatly the kind of thing that cultured people in the latter part of the nineteenth century took poetry to be.

> As one that for a weary space has lain
>   Lull'd by the song of Circe and her wine
>   In gardens near the pale of Proserpine,
> Where that Aeaean isle forgets the main,
> And only the low lutes of love complain,
>   And only shadows of wan lovers pine—
>   As such an one were glad to know the brine
> Salt on his lips, and the large air again—
> So gladly from the songs of modern speech
>   Men turn, and see the stars, and feel the free
>   Shrill wind beyond the close of heavy flowers,
>   And through the music of the languid hours
> They hear like Ocean on a western beach
>   The surge and thunder of the Odyssey.

This is a very representative document. To begin with, there is about the whole thing an atmosphere such as we have learnt to associate with the 'nineties. It is quite in keeping, then, that Swinburne should be very much in evidence : ' gardens near the pale of Proserpine,' ' the low

lutes of love,' 'the close of heavy flowers,' etc.
Morris, too, is there, suggesting a general Pre-
Raphaelite collaboration. Then, as we should
expect in late Victorian poetastry, we are aware of
the pervasive presence of Tennyson. And when
Lang wishes to escape from 'the music of the
languid hours' into the 'larger air' of 'a western
beach' he naturally has recourse to Matthew
Arnold. But in spite of the explicit intention to
end in the larger air, and the success with which
Lang achieves 'the traditional trumpet blast of
the close' (as the reviewers say), it is the music of
the languid hours that predominates in his sonnet.

> We are the music-makers
> And we are the dreamers of dreams,

and if we dream of Homer and of waking up, it is
still dreaming. And there is in the sonnet yet
another presence, that of Keats—the Keats of *La
Belle Dame Sans Merci* (' And only shadows of wan
lovers pine ') which counts for so much in 'the
poetical' of the nineteenth century.

It is not only in the practice of poetasters that
such preconceptions, habits and conventions
assert themselves : they exercise a decisive influence over the use of genuine talent. Poetry
tends in every age to confine itself by ideas of the
essentially poetical which, when the conditions
which gave rise to them have changed, bar the
poet from his most valuable material, the material

that is most significant to sensitive and adequate minds in his own day; or else sensitive and adequate minds are barred out of poetry. Poetry matters because of the kind of poet who is more alive than other people, more alive in his own age. He is, as it were, at the most conscious point of the race in his time. (' He is the point at which the growth of the mind shows itself,' says Mr I. A. Richards.[1]) The potentialities of human experience in any age are realized only by a tiny minority, and the important poet is important because he belongs to this (and has also, of course, the power of communication). Indeed, his capacity for experiencing and his power of communicating are indistinguishable; not merely because we should not know of the one without the other, but because his power of making words express what he feels is indistinguishable from his awareness of what he feels. He is unusually sensitive, unusually aware, more sincere and more himself than the ordinary man can be. He knows what he feels and knows what he is interested in. He is a poet because his interest in his experience is not separable from his interest in words; because, that is, of his habit of seeking by the evocative use of words to sharpen his awareness of his ways of feeling, so making these communicable. And poetry can communicate the actual quality of

[1] *The Principles of Literary Criticism*, p. 61.

experience with a subtlety and precision un-approachable by any other means. But if the poetry and the intelligence of the age lose touch with each other, poetry will cease to matter much, and the age will be lacking in finer awareness. What this last prognostication means it is perhaps impossible to bring home to any one who is not already convinced of the importance of poetry. So that it is indeed deplorable that poetry should so widely have ceased to interest the intelligent.

The mischievousness of the nineteenth-century conventions of ' the poetical ' should by now be plain. They had behind them the prestige of the Romantic achievement and found their sanction in undoubted poetic successes. But as the situation changed and the incidence of stress for the adult sensitive mind shifted, more and more did they tend to get between such a mind and its main concerns. It clearly could not take the day-dream habit seriously, though to cut free from the accompanying conventions and techniques would not be so easy as one might think. The other habits and conventions that have been indicated would be still harder to escape. But they would be equally disabling. For a sensitive adult in the nineteenth century could not fail to be pre-occupied with the changed intellectual back-ground, and to find his main interests inseparable from the modern world. Tennyson did his best.

But, in spite of a great deal of allusion to scientific ideas (' If that hypothesis of theirs be sound '), and in spite of the approval of contemporary savants, his intellectual interests (of which, therefore, we need not discuss the quality) have little to do with his successful poetry, which answers to the account of ' the poetical ' given above. Indeed, there could be no better illustration. To justify his ambition would have taken a much finer intelligence and a much more robust original genius than Tennyson's—much greater strength and courage. He might wrestle solemnly with the ' problems of the age,' but the habits, conventions and techniques that he found congenial are not those of a poet who could have exposed himself freely to the rigours of the contemporary climate. And in this he is representative. It was possible for the poets of the Romantic period to believe that the interests animating their poetry were the forces moving the world, or that might move it. But Victorian poetry admits implicitly that the actual world is alien, recalcitrant and unpoetical, and that no protest is worth making except the protest of withdrawal.

A comparison between any comparable passages of Tennyson and Keats will suggest readily how even Keats,[1] who might at first seem to

---

[1] There is no need to insist on the significance of the revised *Hyperion* and Keats's reasons for the revision.

resist this generalized distinction, may be reconciled with it : Tennyson, in the comparison, will show as literary and Alexandrian, a senior contemporary of the Pre-Raphaelites. His case is well put by *The Palace of Art* : the explicit moral of this poem is that withdrawal will not do ; but when he comes to the moral Tennyson's art breaks down : the poetry belongs to the palace. Pre-Raphaelite art is frankly withdrawn—the appropriate metaphor would suggest something not only beglamoured, but also ritualistic and religiose. Swinburne sings Liberty and Revolution, but it would be difficult to illustrate more forcibly the distinction I have pointed to than by comparing him with Shelley.

The causes of this peculiar other-worldliness of Victorian poetry are sufficiently indicated by Matthew Arnold's recurrent note—his references to

> . . . this strange disease of modern life,
> With its sick hurry, its divided aims,
> Its heads o'ertaxed, its palsied hearts . . .

and to this age that

> had bound
> Our souls in its benumbing round

and

> . . . this iron time
> Of doubts, disputes, distractions, fears.

The frankness of this explicit recognition distinguishes Arnold from among his fellow poets, but it is not enough to constitute the poetic ' criticism of life ' that he desiderated. Alas ! the past was out of date, the future not yet born, and Arnold's response to these conditions does not differ fundamentally from that of his fellows. Whatever reasons of discipline he may give for valuing Wordsworth and the Greeks, it is plain that he frequents them largely as means of escape to ' the freshness of the early world.' His debt to Wordsworth,[1] in fact, is hardly separable from a debt to Coleridge, and he bears much the same kind of relation to these two as Tennyson bears to Coleridge and Keats. If we note further the relation of *Sohrab and Rustum*, for instance, to the ' ineffectual angel ' we shall have a fair idea of Arnold's general relation to the Romantic period. He derives from it in the same kind of way as Tennyson and the Pre-Raphaelites do. This obvious point seems worth dwelling on because he certainly aimed to be a very different kind of poet from these, and his unwitting testimony to the strength of the prevailing atmosphere and conventions is even more striking in his poetry than in his criticism.

I am not thinking of his frankly romantic poems

[1] And of Wordsworth he says : ' The gravest of them, Wordsworth, retired (in Middle-Age phrase) into a monastery. I mean, he plunged himself in the inward life, he voluntarily cut himself off from the modern spirit.'—*Essays in Criticism*. First Series : *Heinrich Heine*.

so much as of his work in the manner of *A Summer Night*, in which he is explicitly concerned with ' this strange disease of modern life.' Except as the explicit occasion of his thin, sweet, meditative melancholy, ' modern life,' ' its sick hurry,' ' its divided aims,' ' its heads o'ertaxed ' are not there. They could have been put there only by genius of the order of Gerard Manley Hopkins— genius, that is, in which technical originality is inseparable from the rare adequacy of mind, sensibility and spirit that it vouches for. Arnold—and we have no reason to say that will and intelligence more than technical abilities were lacking—slips away from ' this uncongenial place, this human life' to moonlight transformations, and the iron time dissolves in wistful, melodious sentiment.

To explain why moonlight appears so often in Arnold's poetry is to explain why, in *Empedocles on Etna*, it should be in the two songs of Callicles that the sap suddenly flows. One of these songs is so obviously significant that a phrase or two from it will be enough to clinch the argument :

> Far, far from here
> The Adriatic breaks in a warm bay . . .
>
> There those two live, far in the Illyrian brakes.
>
> . . . but were rapt, far away . . .

Arnold's manner of evasion distinguishes him from his fellows mainly in the cool, meditative lucidity of his waking dream. In his poems of the English countryside his quest is the Scholar-Gypsy's—sanctuary from the modern world, 'its sick hurry, its divided aims.' And even in poems that do not fall naturally under the head of 'evasion' the sentiment has the same well-bred innocence as always, the same sweet, limpid solemnity : one could hardly have divined in the poet the scourge of the Philistines.

No, Matthew Arnold was not qualified either as critic or poet to give English poetry a new direction. When he predicted that poetry would —advocated that it should—more and more take the place of religion, he intended something very different from an indulging of religious sentiment in a hushed cult of Beauty, a religiose sensuality, a retreat out of the profane world into an exquisite cloistral art ; but this describes fairly enough the development from the Pre-Raphaelites and Swinburne through Pater and Oscar Wilde to the 'nineties.

Where, it might be asked, does Browning come in these generalizations ? His can hardly be described as a poetry of withdrawal. It belongs to the world he lives in, and he lives happily in the Victorian world with no sense of disharmony. But is this altogether by reason of qualities that should recommend a poet ? There are kinds of strength a poet is best without. And it is too plain that Browning would have been less robust if he had been more sensitive and intelligent. He did indeed bring his living interests into his poetry, but it is too plain that they are not the interests of an adult sensitive mind. He did not need to withdraw into a dream-world, because he was able to be a naïve romantic of love and action on the waking plane. If he lived in the Victorian world, it was only as *l'homme moyen sensuel* might live there ; unaware of disharmonies because for him there were none, or, rather, only such as were enough to exhilarate, to give him a joyous sense of physical vitality. It is possible to consider him as a philosophical or psychological poet only by confusing intelligence with delight in the exercise of certain grosser cerebral muscles. When he is a poet he is concerned merely with simple emotions and sentiments : the characteristic corrugation of his surface is merely superficial, and not the expression of a complex sensibility. And yet it was a truly remarkable force that broke as Browning did with the current poetical habits. His use, if only it had been finer, of spoken idiom in verse might have been worth a great deal to later poets : at the end of the century Mr Pound found it worth study. But so inferior a mind and spirit as Browning's could not provide the impulse needed to bring back into poetry the adult intelligence.

As for Meredith, if any one should comment that I have taken no account of him, I can only say that *Modern Love* seems to me the flashy product of unusual but vulgar cleverness working upon cheap emotion : it could serve later poets, if at all, only as a warning.

The further on we go in *The Oxford Book* the more apparent does it become that the age did not make full use of its talent. Who, for instance, would guess from his poetry that William Morris was one of the most versatile, energetic and original men of his time, a force that impinged decisively in the world of practice ? He reserved poetry for his day-dreams.

And if we look through any anthologies covering the last fifty years, it becomes impossible to doubt that distinguished minds that should have gone into poetry have gone elsewhere. It is hard to explain otherwise the dearth of original talent in any form or degree. When original talent of a minor order does manifest itself, as, for instance, in Mr A. E. Housman, or, though the collocation is unfair to Mr Housman, Rupert Brooke, it is apt to exert a disproportionate influence. The books of ' Georgian ' verse abound with tributes, more or less unconscious, to these two poets (not to insist on R. L. Stevenson's part) : indeed it was largely in terms of them that the Victorian bequest of habits and conventions was brought up to date.

But these remained essentially the same, as a perusal of the representative anthology, Mr J. C. Squire's *Selections from Modern Poets*, will show. The modernity manifests itself, for the most part, in a complacent debility ; the robust, full-blooded emotional confidence of the Victorians is lacking, a modest quietness being the Georgian study; and technical liberation, accordingly, takes the form of loose, careless, unconvinced craftsmanship.

To make a fresh start in poetry under such conditions is a desperate matter. It is easy enough to say that poetry must be adequate to modern life, and it has often been said. But nothing has been done until such generalities have been realized in particulars, that is, in the invention of new techniques, and this, in an age when the current conventions will not serve even to provide a start, is something beyond any but a very unusually powerful and original talent. The established habits form a kind of atmosphere from which it is supremely difficult to escape. Mr J. C. Squire, for instance, reviewing in *The Observer* the late Poet Laureate's *The Testament of Beauty*, wrote :

> . . . the old poet has done triumphantly what none of his juniors have managed to do—he has, assisted by courage, a natural sincerity, a belief in the function of poetry, contrived to bring within the borders of a poem, and avoiding flatness, all his feelings, knowledge, speculations, interests, hopes

and fears.   For generations, owing to the reaction of the aesthetic against the new scientific, industrial and largely materialistic world, we have become accustomed to the idea that certain things are ' not poetical,' that a poet can mention a rose, but not a Rolls-Royce, that poetry is a refuge and not an attack, that a poet is a sensitive refugee and not a man facing life, the whole of it, and sounding a clarion call to his more speechless and encumbered fellows.

The first sentence might seem to be in the spirit of this essay, though the phrase ' bring within the borders of a poem ' should put us on our guard. On the next sentence—' we have become accustomed to the idea that certain things are not poetical '—our commentary runs : worse, we have become accustomed to the idea that certain things *are* poetical, e.g. flowers, dawn, dew, birds, love, archaisms and country place-names ; [1] ' that a poet can mention a rose, but not a Rolls-Royce ' —suspicious ; ' that poetry is a refuge and not an attack, that a poet is a sensitive refugee and not a man facing life, the whole of it, and sounding a clarion call '—this will not do : it is plain by now that the critic is trying to put a misconception right by turning it upside-down.   For we are no more justified in demanding that poetry shall be an attack than in demanding that it shall be a refuge.   Indeed, it is very unlikely that a signi-

[1] If it be remarked that the cultivated no longer hold this idea, then the cultivated are reduced to a very small minority indeed.

ficant modern poem will be anything in the nature of a clarion call. The passage betrays a total misconception of the way in which such a poem will exhibit modernity. It will not be by mentioning modern things, the apparatus of modern civilization, or by being about modern subjects or topics. If the Rolls-Royce enters significantly into poetry it will be, perhaps, in some such way as Mr T. S. Eliot suggests [1] when he says that probably the modern's perception of rhythm has been affected by the internal combustion engine. All that we can fairly ask of the poet is that he shall show himself to have been fully alive in our time. The evidence will be in the very texture of his poetry.

Mr Alfred Noyes wrote (is still writing?) a long work in verse, *The Torch-Bearers*, about the succession of great astronomers. A few glances were enough to establish its complete insignificance as poetry. For such an undertaking would have to justify itself in the texture of the verse, by an unmistakable newness of tone, rhythm and imagery, by an utterly unfamiliar ' feel.' Mr Noyes's verse is such as any one with a feeling for language, and a close acquaintance with the poets of the past, could learn to write. On like grounds a subtler performance, Mr Laurence Binyon's *The Sirens*, an ode on the questing spirit of man, must be

---

[1] *Savonarola*, Charlotte Eliot. *Introduction*, xi.

dismissed. The ode has been praised for its technical accomplishment, and in a sense it does exhibit skilled craftsmanship. But the only technique that matters is that which compels words to express an intensely personal way of feeling, so that the reader responds, not in a general way that he knows beforehand to be ' poetical,' but in a precise, particular way that no frequenting of *The Oxford Book* could have made familiar to him. To invent techniques that shall be adequate to the ways of feeling, or modes of experience, of adult, sensitive moderns is difficult in the extreme. Until it has been once done it is so difficult as to seem impossible. One success makes others more probable because less difficult.

That is the peculiar importance of Mr T. S. Eliot. For, though there is, inevitably, a great deal of snobbism in the cult he suffers from, mere snobbism will not account for his prestige among the young. Having a mind unquestionably of rare distinction he has solved his own problem as a poet, and so done more than solve the problem for himself. His influence has been the more effective in that he is a critic as well as a poet, and his criticism and his poetry reinforce each other. It is mainly due to him that no serious poet or critic to-day can fail to realize that English poetry in the future must develop (if at all) along some other line than that running from the Romantics through Tennyson, Swinburne, *A Shropshire Lad*, and Rupert Brooke. He has made a new start, and established new bearings.

To justify these contentions and enforce the general account given above it will be necessary first to make a closer survey of the situation as it was just after the war, before Mr Eliot impinged.

II

The Situation at the End
of World War I

THERE were writing at the end of the war three poets in general acceptance who really were considerable poets : Hardy, Yeats and De la Mare. The last two were read and enjoyed by a comparatively large public ; but Hardy's acceptance has, I shall offer reason for supposing, always been mainly formal (indeed, it was perhaps not yet general) ; so I shall leave him till last.

An account of Mr Yeats's beginnings is an account of the poetical situation in the 'eighties and 'nineties. 'I had learned to think,' he tells us in *Essays*,[1] 'in the midst of the last phase of Pre-Raphaelitism.' And he describes his hostility to the later fashions in painting that his father favoured : 'I had seen the change coming bit by bit and its defence elaborated by young men fresh from the Paris art schools. "We must paint what is in front of us," or "A man must be of his own time," they would say, and if I spoke of Blake or Rossetti they would point out his bad drawing and tell me to admire Carolus Duran and Bastien-

[1] p. 430.

Lepage.'[1] But Mr Yeats knew differently : ' In
my heart I thought that only beautiful things
should be painted, and that only ancient things
and the stuff of dreams were beautiful.'[2]

He had made *Prometheus Unbound* his ' sacred
book,' and had begun to write poetry in imitation
of Shelley and Spenser, whose styles he had ' tried
to mix together ' in a pastoral play. His father
introduced him to *The Earthly Paradise* and he
came to know William Morris personally, and
found him a congenial spirit. When he became
one of the Rhymers' Club along with Johnson,
Dowson and the rest he readily adopted the
current accent and idiom : ' Johnson's phrase
that life is ritual expressed something that was in
all our thoughts.'[3] They had their high-priest—
' If Rossetti was a subconscious influence, and
perhaps the most powerful of all, we looked
consciously to Pater for our philosophy '—and
no one exceeded Mr Yeats in devotion. His early
prose is sometimes comic in its earnestness of
discipleship, in its unctuously cadenced concern
for ' the transmutation of art into life ' :

  . . . tapestry, full of the blue and bronze of
  peacocks, fell over the doors, and shut out all
  history and activity untouched with beauty and
  peace ; and now when I looked at my Crevelli and
  pondered on the rose in the hand of the Virgin,

[1] *Autobiographies*, pp. 141-2.   [2] *Ibid.*, p. 101.
[3] *Ibid.*, p. 372.

wherein the form was so delicate and precise that it seemed more like a thought than a flower, or my Francesca, so full of ghostly astonishment, I knew a Christian's ecstasy without his slavery to rule and custom. . . . I had gathered about me all gods because I believed in none, and experienced every pleasure because I gave myself to none, but held myself apart, individual, indissoluble, a mirror of polished steel.[1]

Yet if, dutifully, he ' noted also many poets and prose-writers of every age, but only those who were a little weary of life, as indeed the greatest have been everywhere,'[2] there is a recurrent theme, a recurrent tone, as, for instance, in his reference to ' simpler days before men's minds, subtilised and complicated by the romantic movement in art and literature, began to tremble on the verge of some unimagined revelation,'[3] that betrays later influences than Pater's. Pater modulates into the pronounced esotericism indicated by the title, *Rosa Alchemica* ; an esotericism that was among the things brought back by Arthur Symons from Paris. The title Yeats gives to his autobiography over these years, *The Trembling of the Veil*, comes from Mallarmé, 'while,' he tells us,[4] ' Villiers de L'Isle Adam had shaped whatever in my *Rosa Alchemica* Pater had not shaped.' It is difficult for us to-day to regard *The Symbolist*

---

[1] *Early Poems and Stories*, p. 466. [2] *Ibid.*, p. 485.
[3] *Ibid.*, p. 471.
[4] *Autobiographies*, p. 395.

Movement in Art and Literature as a work of great importance, but it was such to Yeats and his contemporaries, and this fact, together with the Continental developments that the book offers to reflect, may serve to remind us that the Victorian poetic tradition was not merely a poetic tradition, but a response to the general characteristics of the age.

'I am very religious,' says Mr Yeats in his *Autobiographies*, 'and deprived by Huxley and Tyndall, whom I detested, of the simple-minded religion of my childhood, I had made a new religion, almost an infallible church of poetic tradition, of a fardel of stories, and of personages, and of emotions, inseparable from their first expression, passed on from generation to generation by poets and painters with some help from philosophers and theologians. I wished for a world where I could discover this tradition perpetually ... I had even created a dogma : " Because those imaginary people are created out of the deepest instinct of man, to be his measure and his norm, whatever I can imagine those mouths speaking may be the nearest I can go to truth." ' [1] He hated Victorian science, he tells us,[2] with a 'monkish hate,' and with it he associated the Victorian world. Of *A Doll's House* he says

---

[1] *Autobiographies*, pp. 142-3.
[2] *Ibid.*, p. 101.

characteristically : ' I hated the play ; what was
it but Carolus Duran, Bastien-Lepage, Huxley and
Tyndall all over again ; I resented being invited
to admire dialogue so close to modern educated
speech that music and style were impossible.' [1]
Modern thought and the modern world, being
inimical to the hopes of the heart and the delight
of the senses and the imagination, are repudiated
in the name of poetry—and of life.

This last clause, or the emphasis due to it, distinguishes him from the other Victorian romantics,
distinguishes him too from his fellow esoterics. He
may quote as epigraph to *The Secret Rose* Villiers
de L'Isle Adam's ' As for living, our servants will
do that for us ' ; but there is about his contemplated withdrawal a naïvely romantic, whole-
hearted practical energy that reminds us more of
Shelley than of Rossetti or Pater. ' I planned a
mystical Order,' he tells us in *Autobiographies*,[2]
' which should buy or hire the castle, and keep it
as a place where its members could retire for a
while from the world, and where we might
establish mysteries like those of Eleusis and
Samothrace ; and for ten years to come my most
impassioned thought was a vain attempt to find
philosophy and create ritual for that Order. I had
an unshakable conviction, arising how or whence
I cannot tell, that invisible gates would open as

[1] *Ibid.*, p. 343. [2] *Ibid.*, p. 314.

they opened for Blake, as they opened for Sweden-
borg, as they opened for Boehme, and that this
philosophy would find its manuals of devotion in
all imaginative literature, and set before Irishmen
for special manual an Irish literature which,
though made by many minds, would seem the
work of a single mind, and turn our places of
beauty or legendary association into holy symbols.'
It is not for nothing that the *Prometheus Unbound*
had been his sacred book. And the latter part of
this passage has another significance : Mr Yeats
was an Irishman.

But I anticipate : it is at his poetry that we
should be looking by now ; it is only as they arise
directly out of his poetry that the considerations I
have touched on in the last paragraph matter.
His early verse bears out what he tells us of his
beginnings. William Morris could say with
truth, ' You write my sort of poetry.' [1] This (but
for the last two lines, which suggest Tom Moore)
Morris himself might have written :

> Autumn is over the long leaves that love us,
> And over the mice in the barley sheaves ;
> Yellow the leaves of the rowan above us,
> And yellow the wet wild-strawberry leaves.

> The hour of the waning of love has beset us,
> And weary and worn are our sad souls now ;
> Let us part, ere the season of passion forget us,
> With a kiss and a tear on thy drooping brow.

[1] *Autobiographies*, p. 181.

And Tennyson is behind this (though it could hardly be mistaken for Tennyson) :

> 'Your eyes that once were never weary of mine
> Are bowed in sorrow under pendulous lids,
> Because our love is waning.'
>
> And then she :
> 'Although our love is waning, let us stand
> By the lone border of the lake once more,
> Together in that hour of gentleness
> When the poor tired child, Passion, falls asleep :
> How far away the stars seem, and how far
> Is our first kiss, and ah, how old my heart !'

And this, with its characteristic burden, modulates into Keats and out again :

> The woods of Arcady are dead,
> And over is their antique joy ;
> Of old the world on dreaming fed ;
> Grey Truth is now her painted toy ;
> Yet still she turns her restless head :
> But O, sick children of the world,
> Of all the many changing things
> In dreary dancing past us whirled,
> To the cracked tune that Chronos sings,
> Words alone are certain good.
> Where are now the warring kings,
> Word be-mockers ?—By the Rood
> Where are now the warring kings ?
> An idle word is now their glory,
> By the stammering schoolboy said,
> Reading some entangled story :
> The wandering earth herself may be
> Only a sudden flaming word,
> In clanging space a moment heard,
> Troubling the endless reverie.

．　　．　　．　　．　　．

The long poem which gave its name to the collection of 1889 (his first) might be described as Mr Yeats's *Alastor* and *Endymion*. Its importance is what is indicated by this note : '. . . from the moment when I began the *Wanderings of Usheen* . . . my subject matter became Irish.' Mr Yeats starts in the English tradition, but he is from the outset an Irish poet. The impulse behind the poem is the familiar one. A poet's day-dream could not easily be more cloudy and tenuous than the wistful Elysium of his Irish theme, with its ' dim, pale waters ' and its realms

> Where Aengus dreams from sun to sun
> A Druid dream of the end of days ;

and yet there is a paradoxical energy about the poem that distinguishes it from any of Morris's day-dreams : its pallor and weariness are not the exquisite aesthetic etiolation familiar to the

> Poets with whom I learned my trade,
> Companions of the Cheshire Cheese . . .

For Mr Yeats's Irishness is more than a matter of using Irish themes and an Irish atmosphere. It means that his dream-world is something more than private, personal and literary ; that it has, as it were, an external validation. It gives him the kind of advantage that he has in mind here :

> I filled my mind with the popular beliefs of Ire-
> land. . . . I sought some symbolic language reach-

ing far into the past and associated with familiar names and conspicuous hills that I might not be alone amid the obscure impressions of the senses, . . . or mourned the richness or reality lost to Shelley's *Prometheus Unbound* because he had not discovered in England or in Ireland his Caucasus.[1]

The advantage is put even more significantly here :

I did not believe with my intellect that you could be carried away body and soul, but I believed with my emotions and the belief of the country people made that easy.[2]

In the world created with this kind of sanction he could preserve the ' higher reality ' that his imagination and emotions craved, and without which life seemed worthless. His second collection of poems, *The Rose* (1893), frankly brings the cult of ' Eternal beauty wandering on her way,' with its Red Rose of ' an unimagined revelation,' into the world of Irish lore. But there is still a certain esoteric languor about this phase :

Beauty grown sad with its eternity
Made you of us, and of the dim grey sea ;

and we are again reminded that we are in the 'nineties. (' With a rhythm that still echoed Morris I prayed to the Red Rose.') Here, too, belongs the unfortunate *Innisfree* ; unfortunate, because it is Mr Yeats's most anthologized poem

[1] *Essays*, p. 434.   [2] *Autobiographies*, p. 96.

and recalls to us his own note: 'I tried after the publication of *The Wanderings of Oisin* to write of nothing but emotion, and in the simplest language, and now I have had to go through it all, cutting out or altering passages that are sentimental from lack of thought.' [1]

But with *The Wind Among the Reeds* (1899) the dream-reality takes on a new life, and the poet inhabits it surely. And although the imagery of the Celtic Twilight is heavily worked—'pale,' 'dim,' 'shadowy,' 'desolate,' 'cloud-pale,' 'dream-heavy'—there is no languor or preciosity here. Indeed, 'passion-dimmed' and 'pale fire' are equally important in the vocabulary. For a new force has entered Mr Yeats's poetry—love. It is mainly despairing love, and the poetry is extremely poignant. But for us the essential thing to note is how Mr Yeats turns both exaltation and despair to the heightening of his dream-world, his substitute for the drab quotidian actuality of Huxley, Ibsen and Bastien-Lepage:

> When my arms wrap you round I press
> My heart upon the loveliness
> That long has faded from the world.

It is a perfectly sincere application of the platonic habit, but a very odd one:

> For that pale breast and lingering hand
> Come from a more dream-heavy land,

[1] *Early Poems and Stories*, p. v.

A more dream-heavy hour than this ;
And when you sigh from kiss to kiss
I hear white Beauty sighing, too,
For hours when all must fade like dew,
But flame on flame, and deep on deep,
Throne over throne where in half sleep,
Their swords upon their iron knees,
Brood her high lonely mysteries.

—Transcendental Beauty, the mystical reality, belongs to a more dream-heavy hour even than that of the poetry, which is thus the dream of a dream. The syntax of the passage, curiously elusive as it is, suggests the equivocal status of Yeats's ' reality.' It is more than a literary fiction ; love and the Irish background (' I believed with my emotions and the belief of the country people made that easy ') enabled him to make it so. The resulting poetry has a fresh unliterary spontaneity comparable to that of Shelley's, but a spontaneity that has behind it Victorian literary sophistication instead of Wordsworth and the French Revolution, and so is the more remarkable an achievement. Yet everywhere there is a recognition, implicit in the shifting, cloudy unseizableness of the imagery, that this ' reality ' must be illusory, and that even if it could be reached it would leave human longing unslaked. And this recognition is subtly turned into a strength : it validates, as it were, the idealizing fanaticism of the poetry and counterpoises the obsession with the transcen-

dental, just as the exaltations and despairs of love
are counterpoised by the sense that

> . . . time and the world are ever in flight;
> And love is less kind than the grey twilight,
> And hope is less dear than the dew of the morn.

The poetry of *The Wind Among the Reeds*, then,
is a very remarkable achievement : it is, though a
poetry of withdrawal, both more subtle and more
vital than any pure product of Victorian romanticism. We might, as bearing on the strength it was
to Mr Yeats to be Irish, note further that with the
Irish element in the poetry was associated a public
and practical aim. Early and long service in the
cause of a national renaissance, and, above all, of
a national theatre, might be expected to turn even
a poet of the Victorian dream-world into something else ; and Mr Yeats devoted to the Irish
cause rare qualities of character and intelligence.
Yet his resolute attempt upon the drama serves
mainly to bring out the prepotence of the tradition he started in. His plays repudiate the actual
world as essentially as his incantatory lyrics and
his esoteric prose repudiate it. ' As for living,
our servants will do that for us '—the epigraph
might cover all three. A drama thus devoted to
a ' higher reality ' of this kind could hardly
exhibit the dramatic virtues.

How insidious was the atmosphere that poets of
his time breathed comes out in his critical writings.

'Tragic art,' he will tell us in a discussion of poetic drama,[1] 'passionate art, the drowner of dykes, moves us by setting us to reverie, by alluring us almost to the intensity of trance.' And so obviously acute is the critical intelligence at work that we try to find much virtue in that ' intensity.' Yet ' reverie ' and ' trance ' are dangerous words, and in the critic who announces that ' All art is dream '[2] we fear the worst. 'Drama,' he will tell us again,[3] ' is a means of expression . . . and the dramatist is as free to choose where he has a mind to, as the poet of *Endymion*, or as the painter of Mary Magdalene at the door of Simon the Pharisee. So far from the discussion of our interests and the immediate circumstances of our life being the most moving to the imagination, it is what is old and far-off that stirs us the most deeply.' Reading this, we may applaud the challenge to Shaw and Ibsen, but we more than suspect the kind of dream he has in mind. Indeed, we know, for the bent is inveterate. ' Every writer,' he says,[4] ' even every small writer, who has belonged to the great tradition, has had his dream of an impossibly noble life, and the greater he is, the more does it seem to plunge him into some beautiful or bitter reverie.' This comes from an essay on Synge, and of Synge's rhythm he says :[5] ' It is essential, for it

---

[1] *Essays*, p. 303.   [2] *Ibid.*, p. 354.   [3] *Ibid.*, p. 352.
[4] *Ibid.*, p. 376.   [5] *Ibid.*, p. 371.

perfectly fits the drifting emotion, the dreaminess, the vague yet measureless desire, for which he would create a dramatic form. It blurs definition, clear edges, everything that comes from the will, it turns imagination from all that is of the present, like a gold background in a religious picture, and it strengthens in every emotion whatever comes to it from far off, from brooding memory and dangerous hope.'

Mr Yeats the dramatist, that is, remains the poet who had 'learned to think in the midst of the last phase of Pre-Raphaelitism.' He differs from the Victorian romantics in the intensity with which he seeks his 'higher reality.' This difference we have attributed to his being Irish; but it will not do to let this explanation detract from his rare distinction of mind and spirit. 'I had an invincible conviction . . . that the gates would open as they opened for Blake . . .'—this is not the anaemic reverie of Victorian romanticism: to nurse a luxury of defeat was not in Mr Yeats's character; he was too strong and alive. He fought, paradoxical as it may seem, for victory, and it was not through any lack of intelligence or contempt for it that he found such a Quixotry possible. 'The dream-world of Morris,' he writes,[1] 'was as much the antithesis of daily life as with other men of genius, but he was never

[1] *Autobiographies*, p. 175.

conscious of the antithesis and so knew nothing of intellectual suffering.' Mr Yeats knew much of intellectual suffering, for the antithesis was terribly present to him : he had a magnificent mind, and less than the ordinary man's capacity for self-deception. 'It is so many years before one can believe enough in what one feels even to know what the feeling is,' he notes,[1] exemplifying that rare critical self-awareness of which the signs abound in his *Autobiographies* and *Essays*. 'I ceased to read modern books that were not books of imagination,' he reports ;[2] but he read these last, one might almost say, in a scientific spirit. Indeed, his dealings with spiritualism, magic, theosophy, dream and trance were essentially an attempt to create an alternative science. The science of Huxley and Tyndall he had rejected in the name of imagination and emotion, but he had an intelligence that would not be denied. He exhibits for us the inner struggle of the nineteenth-century mind in an heroic form— heroic, and, because of the inevitable frustration and waste, tragic. 'From the moment when these speculations grew vivid,' he tells us,[3] 'I had created for myself an intellectual solitude.'

We may relate to this lonely struggle a remark-able change that manifests itself in Mr Yeats's

[1] *Ibid.*, p. 127.   [2] *Ibid.*, p. 328.   [3] *Ibid.*, p. 326.

poetry when we compare *The Wind Among the Reeds* (1899) with *The Green Helmet* (1912). It is hard to believe that the characteristic verse of the later volume comes from the same hand as that of the earlier. The new verse has no incantation, no dreamy, hypnotic rhythm ; it belongs to the actual, waking world, and is in the idiom and movement of modern speech. It is spare, hard and sinewy and in tone sardonic, expressing the bitterness and disillusion of a man who has struggled and been frustrated :

> The fascination of what's difficult
> Has dried the sap out of my veins, and rent
> Spontaneous joy and natural content
> Out of my heart.

It is true that the struggles he specifies here belong to the practical world, to ' this blind, bitter land ' :

> My curse on plays
> That have to be set up in fifty ways,
> On the day's war with every knave and dolt,
> Theatre business, management of men.

But this is not the whole tale ; and if it is time that has brought this maturity, there are reasons why this maturity should be so sour.

> Though leaves are many, the root is one ;
> Through all the lying days of my youth
> I swayed my leaves and flowers in the sun ;
> Now I may wither into the truth

runs a quatrain headed *The Coming of Wisdom with Time*.   Actuality has conquered :

> The holy centaurs of the hill are vanished ;
> I have nothing but the embittered sun ;
> Banished heroic mother moon and vanished,
> And now that I have come to fifty years
> I must endure the timid sun.

It is like an awakening out of drugs, a disintoxication ; the daylight seems thin and cruel.   He recognizes the real world, but it is too late ; his strength has been wasted, and habit forbids readjustment.

> But I grow old among dreams,
> A weather-worn, marble triton
> Among the streams.

The poem this last comes from has for title *Men Improve with the Years*, which suggests well enough Mr Yeats's peculiar bitterness, a bitterness mingled with scorn for humanity.[1]

Nevertheless, the poetry of this later phase is a remarkable positive achievement : Mr Yeats was strong enough to force a triumph out of defeat. He speaks of a beauty

> . . . won
> From bitterest hours,

[1] Cf.
> We had fed the heart on fantasies,
> The heart's grown brutal from the fare,
> More substance in our enmities
> Than in our love ;
>
> *The Tower*, p. 27.

and it is this he serves instead of the cloudy
glamour of the *Celtic Twilight* ; a

> . . . beauty like a tightened bow, a kind
> That is not natural in an age like this.

The verse, in its rhythm and diction, recognizes
the actual world, but holds against it an ideal of
aristocratic fineness. It is idiomatic, and has the
run of free speech, being at the same time proud,
bare and subtle. To pass from the earlier verse
to this is something like passing from Campion to
Donne. The parallel, indeed, is not so random as
it might seem. At any rate, Donne's name in
connection with a poet capable of passionate
intellectual interests, who from such a start
achieved such a manner, leads us to reflect that if
the poetic tradition of the nineteenth century had
been less completely unlike the Metaphysical
tradition Mr Yeats might have spent less of his
power outside poetry. The speculation is perhaps
idle, but it calls attention to the way in which his
verse developed into something that has the
equivalent of certain seventeenth-century qualities. His use of the idiom and rhythm of speech
is not all :

> Plato thought nature but a spume that plays
> Upon a ghostly paradigm of things ;
> Solider Aristotle played the taws
> Upon the bottom of a king of kings ;

> World-famous golden-thighed Pythagoras
> Fingered upon a fiddle stick or strings
> What a star sang and careless Muses heard :
> Old clothes upon old sticks to scare a bird.

—This (and the context more than bears out the promise of flexibility and variety of tone) is surely rather like seventeenth-century ' wit ' ; more like it than anything we expect to find in modern verse outside the work of certain post-war poets— poets who exhibit no completer escape from the Victorian poetical. The volume it comes from, indeed, appeared after the war. But *The Tower* (1928) merely develops the manner of *The Green Helmet* (1912), *Responsibilities* (1914), and *The Wild Swans at Coole* (1919).

In *The Tower* Mr Yeats achieves a kind of ripeness in disillusion. The scorn so pervasive before is gone : his tragic horror at the plight of Ireland (as, for instance, in *Meditations in Time of Civil War*) is something different and more generous. There is indeed bitterness, but it is not the sterile kind. His raging against

> Decrepit age that has been tied to me
> As to a dog's tail

goes with a sense of ardent vitality :

> . . . Never had I more
> Excited, passionate, fantastical
> Imagination, nor an ear and eye
> That more expected the impossible ;

and the excitement is as apparent as the bitterness in this poetry of the last phase. Each gives value to the other. He is capable of excitement, for instance, about the 'abstract things' that he describes as a *pis aller*. He turns with a pang from the varied 'sensual music' of the world, but he is drawn positively towards the 'monuments of unaging intellect':

> An aged man is but a paltry thing,
> A tattered coat upon a stick, unless
> Soul clap its hands and sing, and louder sing
> For every tatter in its mortal dress.

This (though there is always an ironical overtone) is the voice of one who knows intellectual passion. He does not deceive himself about what he has lost, but the regret itself becomes in the poetry something positive. His implications, in short, are very complex; he has achieved a difficult and delicate sincerity, an extraordinarily subtle poise.

What, then, it might be asked after this account of Mr Yeats's achievement, is there to complain of? Does it really show that the tradition in the nineteenth century might with advantage have been other than it was? If he had to struggle with uncongenial circumstances, has not every great artist had to do so; and did he not, by admission, make triumphs of them? Mr Yeats himself gives the answer in the bitter sense of waste he expresses characteristically, in the latest work as elsewhere. His poetry is little more than a marginal comment on the main activities of his life. No one can read his *Autobiographies* and his *Essays* without being struck by the magnificent qualities of intelligence and character he exhibits. His insight shows itself in his analysis of his own case, an analysis that suggests at the same time the complete achievement he was fated to miss : ' In literature,' he wrote in 1906,[1] ' partly from the lack of that spoken word which knits us to the normal man, we have lost in personality, in our delight in the whole man—blood, imagination, intellect, running together—but have found a new delight in essences, in states of mind, in pure imagination, in all that comes to us most easily in elaborate music.' And we find him remarking in *Autobiographies* [2] ' how small a fragment of our own nature can be brought to perfect expression, nor that even but with great toil, in a much divided civilisation.' Again,[3] by quoting his own verse, he explicitly relates the general reflection to his own case : ' Nor did I understand as yet how little that Unity [of Being], however wisely sought, is possible without a Unity of Culture

---

[1] *Essays*, p. 330. Cf. ' Donne could be as metaphysical as he pleased . . . because he could be as physical as he pleased.'—*Autobiographies*, p. 402.

[2] p. 364.

[3] *Autobiographies*, p. 436.

in class or people that is no longer possible
at all.

> The fascination of what's difficult
> Has dried the sap out of my veins, and rent
> Spontaneous joy and natural content
> Out of my heart.'

At this point it might be commented that
Mr Yeats turns out an unfortunate witness to
have called. What he testifies against is not the
poetic tradition, but the general state of civilization and culture; a state which, he contends,
makes waste inevitable for the sensitive. But he
implies nothing against holding that if the poetic
tradition had been different, as it might very well
have been, he might have brought more of himself to expression. Writing of the early Synge he
says [1] significantly : ' . . . the only language that
interested him was that conventional language of
modern poetry which has begun to make us all
weary. I was very weary of it, for I had finished
The Secret Rose, and felt how it had separated my
imagination from life, sending my Red Hanrahan,
who should have trodden the same roads with
myself, into some undiscoverable country.' It is
true that he successfully dropped this ' conventional language of modern poetry ' ; but early
habits of mind and sensibility are not so easily

[1] *Essays*, p. 370.

dropped.   The incidental confession he makes in a later poem—

> I have no speech but symbol, the pagan speech I
>   made
> Amid the dreams of youth——

has much significance.   For 'symbol' in his technical sense—symbol drawn from his cult of magic and the Hermetic sciences—is commonly felt to be an unsatisfactory element in his later verse, and to come from an unfortunate habit of mind.   And his magic and occultism, of course, are the persistent and intense expression of the bent that expressed itself first of all in the ' conventional language of modern poetry ' :

> — . . . The abstract joy,
> The half read wisdom of daemonic images,
> Suffice the aging man as once the growing boy.

Disillusion and waste were indeed inevitable ; but not in the form in which Mr Yeats suffered them.   They might have been more significant. For Victorian romanticism was not the only possible answer to those modern conditions that Mr Yeats deplores.   If it were, poetry would cease to matter.   Adult minds could no longer take it seriously.   Losing all touch with the finer consciousness of the age it would be, not only irresponsible, but anaemic, as, indeed, Victorian poetry so commonly is.   Mr Yeats's career, then, magnificent as the triumph was that he compelled

out of defeat, is a warning. It illustrates the
special disability of the poet in the last century,
and impressively bears out my argument about
the poetic tradition. And it cannot be repeated.
No Englishman in any case could have profited
by the sources of strength open to Mr Yeats as an
Irishman, and no such source is open to any one
now. No serious poet could propose to begin
again where Mr Yeats began.

Both Mr Yeats's genius and the advantages he
enjoyed as an Irishman are brought out by comparison with Walter de la Mare. Mr de la Mare
says of children, ' Between their dream and their
reality looms no impassable abyss '; and his
poetry is peculiarly related to childhood. He has
written poems from the child's consciousness;
poems that recapture the child's mentality as he
describes it. These are very remarkable; but
still more interesting from our point of view are
the poems (by far the greater in number) in which
the adult is present.

> Very old are the woods;
>   And the buds that break
> Out of the briar's boughs,
>   When March winds wake,
> So old with their beauty are—
>   Oh, no man knows
> Through what wild centuries
>   Roves back the rose.

—The well-known poem this comes from is

frankly a piece of enchantment; the rhythm is a potent spell, and the appropriate hush establishes itself in the first line. Any one faced with describing the effect would set down 'glamour,' 'mystery,' 'wonder' among the key-words. Perhaps only a reader familiar with Mr de la Mare would note that in this first stanza he is playing in particular upon reminiscences of the Sleeping Beauty. The suggestion may seem unnecessary, but it is not random, and it serves to point the observation that in general, however serious his intention, he is exploiting the fairy-tale stratum of experience.

He is often more urgently concerned with Time than in *All That's Past*, but he always uses, with varying degrees of subtlety, the same means of enchantment. 'Time dreams'[1] in his poetry:

> Our hearts stood still in the hush
> Of an age gone by.

He thus uses

> The skill of words to sweeten despair
> Of finding consolation where
> Life has but one dark end.

He is frank about the aim of his poetry and about his relations with childhood. He finds the modern world, with its science and its civilization,

---

[1] See *The Unchanging*.

as uncongenial as Mr Yeats found it. It is impossible either to conquer it or to become reconciled with it, so—

> What can the tired heart say
> Which the wise of the world have made dumb?
> Save to the lonely dreams of a child,
> Return again, come!

His poetry, then, is by admission a poetry of withdrawal, cultivating a special poetical ' reality ' : his world of dreams, nourished upon memories of childhood, is for him the intrinsically poetical.

But this is too simple an account of Mr de la Mare. It suggests that he is always frank about what he is doing ; or rather, it does not suggest the subtlety that attends upon the frankness. An adult can hardly, even in his poetry, always turn his back so directly and simply upon the world. Mr de la Mare, as a matter of fact, is a great deal given to the contemplation of that human plight which desolates him. There is something odd about the manner of contemplation. He exhibits a characteristic subtlety that can fairly be called legerdemain : he produces, by the surreptitious suggestions of his verse, an effect contradictory to what he says. ' His utterance,' says Mr I. A. Richards,[1] who acutely diagnoses the trick, ' in spite of his words, becomes not at all a recognition of this indifference [of the Universe to human

[1] *Science and Poetry*, p. 71.

desires], but voices instead an impulse to turn away, to forget it, to seek shelter in the warmth of his own familiar thicket of dream, not to stay out in the wind.' He has formed habits that make impossible such a frank recognition of the human plight as he seems to offer. The apparent recognition is not the frankness it pretends to be but an insidious enhancement of the spell, which is the more potent to soothe and lull when it seems to be doing the opposite. Mr de la Mare's poetry cultivates subtler (and more dangerous) illusions than it professes.

The working of this surreptitious magic may be readily examined in *The Ghost*, a poem which contrasts conveniently with Hardy's *The Voice*. The explicit burden is the emptiness of utter loss :

> Nought but vast sorrow was there—
> The sweet cheat gone.

'Sweet cheat' fairly describes the poem. The sleight begins in the first stanza, and by the end of the second the spell is established. The reference to ' dreams ' is not as negative as it pretends to be. The grave when described as ' the roots of the dark thorn ' suggests dew, fragrance and fairies rather than death and decay. The fairy-tale atmosphere is fortified obviously by the second stanza, so that, though the third is glamourless enough, a strong habituation in the reader still

survives to seize on any magic potentialities.
They come in a most interesting way :

> Silence.   Still faint on the porch
> Brake the flames of the stars.

The night-sky starlit (exemplifying the general
tendency of his imagery to repeat itself far too
much) recurs with notable frequency in Mr de la
Mare's verse : it lends itself peculiarly to his
habitual legerdemain. Here its open function is
to suggest the desolate, pygmy helplessness of
man. But another set of associations also hangs
about the starlit night ; those avowed, for example, in *The Unchanging* : enchantment, mystery,
elves, fragrance, dew ; and these make their effect
here. In such ways is produced the equivocal
sweet poignancy characteristic of Mr de la Mare.

   To be able to work so insidious a spell as
successfully as he does in his best poetry is to be
in some measure a victim of it oneself. How
unsatisfactory an addiction it is his own history as
a poet suggests. His last serious volume of verse,
The Veil, came out as long ago as 1921, and its
contents seem to explain adequately why no later
volume has followed. In *The Veil* the poignancy
turns into a duller, heavier desolation ; the dream
takes on a nightmare quality ; and the unwhole-
someness of the fantasy-habit is, implicitly and
explicitly, admitted. It is as if the disastrous
consequences of drug-addiction were being recog-

nized. Life seems now not tragic but flat and empty. 'I have come to the end of things,' says a character in one of his stories,[1] describing this state. 'For me, the spirit, the meaning—whatever you like to call it—has vanished, gone clean out of the world, out of what we call reality.' And this character plays with the idea of a pair of enchanted spectacles that should give meaning back to the world. But the magic has ceased to work for Mr de la Mare. In such a poem as *The Familiar* he laments his estrangement from the spirit that wove the spell ; and the spell in his poetry is visibly failing. When he essays a new kind of poetry that shall be solidly based in the actual world (see, for instance, *In the Dock*) he is capable of a gross badness shocking in so exquisite a poet. It seems, then, reasonable to suppose that he will not produce much more good poetry.

Since *The Veil* he has devoted himself to prose. His more successful stories derive from the same kind of impulse as his poetry. But the sharp critical awareness that guides him in his poetry does not function here : his main talent is not engaged. And success (or the absence of it) in prose is not the decisive local manifestation that it is in poetry. His continuing to seek the 'poetical' in prose has little bearing on our conclusion regarding the poet.

[1] *The Connoisseur*, p. 142.

He has written a remarkable bulk of exquisite minor poetry (admirably appreciated by Mr Middleton Murry in *Countries of the Mind*); but even this cloys, and the moral of his career can hardly be doubtful. He is the belated last poet of the Romantic tradition, and is already as remote as Poe from the present of poetry.

The Veil, where Mr de la Mare recognizes the vanity of his poetic evasions, shows curious traces of Hardy's influence. It is as if, in his straits, he had gone for help to the poet most unlike himself, strong where he is weak. For Hardy may be so described : in their characteristic manners, the two poets offer an extreme contrast. The contrast comes out fairly in the two poems already suggested for comparison ; for if *The Ghost* does not, as *The Voice* does, represent the very summit of its author's achievement, it is nevertheless characteristic. *The Voice* really does evoke the emptiness of utter loss, exhibiting ,that purity of recognition which is Hardy's strength. His verse has no incantation : it does what it says, and presents barely the fact recognized by a mind more than commonly responsible and awake.

The omission of Hardy from my summing-up of the nineteenth century has no doubt provoked some comment. Here, surely, is a Victorian poet who wrote great poetry evincing an intense concern, not with a world of day-dreams, but with the human situation as it appeared in the light of modern thought. And no one would accuse him of optimistic or sentimental evasions or insincerities. But Hardy did not begin to publish poetry until the very end of the last century, when some of his best still remained to write; so that, even if he had been a potential influence, he did not impinge until it was too late. By then the stresses incident to the most sensitive and aware had shifted and altered. Hardy is now seen to be truly a Victorian—a Victorian in his very pessimism, which implies positives and assurances that have vanished. He inhabits a solid world, with the earth firm under his feet. He knows what he wants, what he values and what he is. It is characteristic that he should end one of his best poems, *After a Journey*, a poem of retrospect in old age:

> . . . bring me here again!
> I am just the same as when
> Our days were a joy, and our paths through flowers.

Compare this poem, or any other of Hardy's best, with, say, one of Edward Thomas's (a representative modern sensibility), and Hardy's solidity appears archaic.

Hardy is a naïve poet of simple attitudes and outlook. The attitudes and outlook were the product of what Mr I. A. Richards in *Science and Poetry* [1] calls 'the neutralization of nature.'

[1] See particularly sections V. and VII.

Hardy's greatness lies in the integrity with which he accepted the conclusion, enforced, he believed, by science, that nature is indifferent to human values, in the completeness of his recognition, and in the purity and adequacy of his response. He was betrayed into no heroic postures. He felt deeply and consistently, he knew what he felt, and, in his best poems, communicated it perfectly. But there was little in his technique that could be taken up by younger poets, and developed in the solution of their own problems. His originality was not of the kind that goes with a high degree of critical awareness : it went, indeed, with a naïve conservatism. 'In his opinion,' reports Mr Robert Graves in his superb autobiography, *Goodbye to All That*, ' *vers libre* could come to nothing in England. " All we can do is to write on the old themes in the old styles, but try to do a little better than those who went before us." ' And again : ' " Why ! " he said, " I have never in my life taken more than three, or perhaps four drafts for a poem. I am afraid of it losing its freshness." ' [1] It is all in keeping with this precritical innocence that his great poems should be only a very small proportion of his abundant output.

[1] ' His taste in literature was certainly most unexpected. Once when Lawrence [T. E.] had ventured to say something disparaging against Homer's *Iliad* he protested : " Oh, but I admire the *Iliad* greatly. Why, it's in the *Marmion* class ! " Lawrence could not at first believe that Hardy was not making a little joke.'—*Goodbye to All That*, p. 378.

How small a proportion this is does not seem to be generally recognized : his rank as a major poet rests upon a dozen poems. These are lost among a vast bulk of verse interesting only by its oddity and idiosyncrasy, and as illustrating the habits that somehow become strength in his great poetry. The main impulse behind his verse is too commonly the mere impulse to write verse : 'Any little old song will do,' [1] as he says. And, often to the lilt of popular airs, with a gaucherie compounded of the literary, the colloquial, the baldly prosaic, the conventionally poetical, the pedantic and the rustic, he industriously turns out his despondent anecdotes, his ' life's little ironies,' and his meditations upon a deterministic universe and the cruel accident of sentience. The inveterate bent is significant, even if the verse has little intrinsic value : Hardy's great poetry is a triumph of character. Now and then, when he is deeply moved (the impulse is usually a poignant memory), this bent and these habits suddenly appear as strength, the oddity becomes an intensely personal virtue. *The Voice*, for instance, seems to start dangerously with a crude popular lilt, but this is turned into a subtle movement by the prosaic manner of the content, a manner that elsewhere would have been Hardy's characteristic gaucherie :

[1] ' *Any little old song* ' (*Human Shows and Far Phantasies*).

Can it be you that I hear?   Let me view you, then,
Standing as when I drew near to the town
Where you would wait for me: yes, as I knew you then,
Even to the original air-blue gown!

By the end of this second stanza the bare matter-of-fact statement has already subdued the rhythm; the shift of stress on the rime (' view you then,' ' knew you thén ') has banished the jingle from it. In the next stanza we have an instance of his odd word-coinages:

Or is it only the breeze, in its listlessness
Travelling across the wet mead to me here,
You being ever dissolved to existlessness,
Heard no more again far or near?

—' Existlessness ' (which he afterwards, and, I think, unfortunately, changed to ' wan wistless-ness ') is a questionable word, a characteristic eccentricity of invention; and yet here it sounds right. The touch that there may still be about the poem of what would normally have been rustic stiffness serves as a kind of guarantee of integrity. And then there is the exquisite modula-tion into the last stanza.[1]

Hardy needed a strong, immediately personal impulse before he could transform his innocent awkwardness in this way. The mere impulse to versify reflections and anecdotes in illustration of his ' philosophy ' was not enough. His great

[1] I am assuming that every one interested enough to read this account will have opened the volume of Hardy at the poem.

poems, as a rule, start immediately out of his own remembered past, and are particular evocations of utter loss, the blindness of chance, the poignancy of love and its helplessness, and the cruelty of time. Such poems are *After a Journey, The Voice, The Self-Unseeing, A Broken Appointment, Neutral Tones, During Wind and Rain*. That the setting, explicit or implied, is generally rural is a point of critical significance. Hardy was a countryman, and his brooding mind stayed itself habitually upon the simple pieties, the quiet rhythms and the immemorial ritual of rustic life.

It is very largely in terms of the absence of these, or of any equivalent, that the environment of the modern poet must be described. Urban conditions, a sophisticated civilization, rapid change and the mingling of cultures have destroyed the old rhythms and habits, and nothing adequate has taken their place. The result is a sense, apparent in the serious literature of the day, that meaning and direction have vanished. These conditions, of course, partly account for the weakness of poetry in recent times : we should not expect them to favour a confident flow of creative power. But they are far from accounting wholly for the plight revealed by the Georgian anthologies and the latter part of *The Oxford Book of Victorian Verse*. Mr Eliot's poetry is proof enough of this.

The almost unvarying way in which anthologists choose from his insignificant poems and
leave out the great ones suggests that Hardy's
repute is mainly conventional, and that he is little
read, or, at any rate, little appreciated. It would
no doubt be possible to point to his influence in
contemporary verse, but a Hardy who can blend
with the *Shropshire Lad* is not important.

Besides Hardy, Yeats and de la Mare there was
supposed to be a galaxy of Georgian poets. The
Georgian movement may fairly be considered as
a ' movement,' since it can be considered as little
else. ' There was,' writes [1] its promoter, E. M.,
' a general feeling among the younger poets that
modern English poetry was very good, and sadly
neglected by readers.' There may very reasonably have been a general feeling that the Victorian
Age was now well over, and that it was time we
had a modern English poetry. At any rate, E. M.
and his friends did their best, and were warmly
supported by the public; *Georgian Poetry*, 1911-
1912, the first of the series, came out, and ' its
success outran our wildest hopes.' From then on,
in general acceptance, the age was a poetical one.
The ' corporate flavour ' of the movement is
admirably described by Mr Middleton Murry in
an article [2] that he wrote in 1919. There is no

---

[1] *Memoir* (p. lxxvi) prefixed to *The Collected Poems of Rupert Brooke*.
This *Memoir* tells one a great deal about the spirit of the movement.
[2] *Present Condition of English Poetry* in *Aspects of Literature*.

need to examine again the false simplicity that he diagnoses ; but it may be worth remarking in this connection that a glance through *Poems of To-day* (two anthologies unfortunately much used in schools) suggests that R. L. Stevenson was a stronger influence as a poet than one would have thought possible. The *Shropshire Lad*, on the other hand, was a predestined victim.

But although Mr Drinkwater may perhaps claim to be the representative Georgian poet the dominating figure is Rupert Brooke. Brooke had considerable personal force and became himself an influence. He energized the Garden-Suburb ethos with a certain original talent and the vigour of a prolonged adolescence. His verse exhibits a genuine sensuousness rather like Keats's (though more energetic) and something that is rather like Keats's vulgarity with a Public School accent. It is odd to be reminded that he was once thought ' complex '—almost a metaphysical poet :

> Mrs Cornford tried to engage me in a controversy over the book—she and her school. They are known as the Heart-criers, because they believe all poetry ought to be short, simple, naïve, and a cry from the heart ; the sort of thing an inspired only child might utter if it was in the habit of posing to its elders. They object to my poetry as unreal, affected, complex, ' literary,' and full of long words.[1]

The uneasiness betrayed here at the prevailing

[1] *Memoir*, p. lxviii.

simplesse is not the same thing as complete awareness and immunity. And Brooke's ' complexity '
amounts to little more than an inhibiting adolescent self-consciousness in an ironical disguise.
In its extremer forms it is painfully embarrassing.
The marks of his enthusiasm for Donne (who was
then ' coming in ') serve only to bring out how
safe he was from such an influence. He borrows,
for instance, ' scattering-bright ' [1] and converts it
to the vague uses of his adjectival glamour—' the
inenarrable godhead of delight.' The adolescent
zest with which he pursues this glamour (the
intrinsically ' poetical ') has, together with his
adolescent yearning for a maternal bosom where

Surely a shamed head may bow down at length,

ensured him a real popularity unknown to
the other Georgians (except the present Poet
Laureate).

He was in the first days of his fame notorious
for his ' unpleasantness,' his ' realism.'

I'm (of course) unrepentant about the ' unpleas-
ant ' poems. I don't claim great credit for the *Chan-
nel Passage* : but the point of it was (or should
have been !) ' serious.' There are common and
sordid things—situations or details—that may suddenly bring all tragedy, or at least the brutality of
actual emotions, to you. I rather grasp relievedly
at them, after I've beaten vain hands in the rosy
mists of poets' experiences.[2]

[1] See *Beauty and Beauty* and Donne's *Aire and Angels*.
[2] *Memoir*, p. lxvii.

—But he was always, as he reveals here, poetical at heart : the last sentence is especially betraying.

A grasping in a like spirit at common and sordid things was frequent among Georgian poets : there was a determination to modernize poetry, and bring it closer to life. The present Poet Laureate above all earned notoriety by his ' realism.' He crossed Yeats with Kipling, and managed to reconcile the sordid facts of life with the rosy mists of poets' experiences. If we bracket him with Flecker who, standing for Parnassian perfection, was supposed to stand apart, we make, from our point of view, the adequate comment on both : no serious effort of readjustment is involved in passing from one to the other. Later more subtle attempts to escape from the poetical were made by Mr J. C. Squire, but they served only to call attention to the bankruptcy of tradition and the difficulty of a new start.

Opposed to these there is a group, including some respected names, that might be called academic. They are conscientious and persevering, and one of them at least has been admitted to immortality in the *Oxford* series ; but it is hard to believe that they are read. Then there is the central group of Georgian poets who specialize in country sentiment and the pursuit of Beauty in her more chaste and subtle guises. Mr Middleton Murry has dealt with them adequately in the

E

article already mentioned, and there is no need to enumerate them here. But two poets commonly included deserve to be distinguished from the group: Mr Edmund Blunden, because he has some genuine talent and is an interesting case, and Edward Thomas, an original poet of rare quality, who has been associated with the Georgians by mischance.

The Shepherd, Mr Blunden's first mature book of verse, marked him out from the crowd as a poet who, though he wrote about the country, drew neither upon the *Shropshire Lad* nor upon the common stock of Georgian country sentiment. There was also in his poems, for all the rich rusticity, the homespun texture that is their warrant, a frank literary quality: Mr Blunden was concerned with art; he was making something. And—what gives them their interest for us—corresponding to this quality in the form there appeared to be something in the intention behind: out of the traditional life of the English countryside, especially as relived in memories of childhood, Mr Blunden was creating a world—a world in which to find refuge from adult distresses; above all, one guessed, from memories of the war.

The later volumes, *English Poems*, *Retreat* and *Near and Far*, confirm this conjecture. The peculiar poise that constituted Mr Blunden's dis-

tinction has proved difficult to maintain. On the
one hand, the stress behind the pastoral quiet
becomes explicit in poems dealing with mental
conflict, hallucination and war-experience; on
the other, the literary quality becomes, in other
poems, more pronounced, and takes the form of
frank eighteenth-century echoes, imitations and
reminiscences :

> From *Grongar Hill* the thrush and flute awoke,
> And Green's mild sibyl chanted from her oak,
> Along the vale sang Collins' hamlet bell.

Mr Blunden's retreat is to an Arcadia that is rural
England seen, not only through memories of
childhood, but through poetry and art (see *A
Favourite Scene recalled on looking at Birket Foster's
Landscapes*).[1] Eighteenth-century meditative pastoral is especially congenial to him; he takes over
even the nymphs and their attendant classicalities.
On the other hand, he attempts psychological
subtleties, and deals directly with his unease, his
inner tensions, instead of implying them, as
before, in the solidity of his created world. And
it becomes plain that he is attempting something
beyond him. The earlier method suited his
powers and enabled him better to harmonize his
various interests. There was something satisfying
about the dense richness of his pastoral world,
with its giant puff-balls and other evocations of

[1] *Retreat.*

animistic fancy instead of nymphs and naiads. But in the later volumes there is a serious instability in Mr Blunden's art. The visionary gleam, the vanished glory, the transcendental suggestion remain too often vague, the rhythms stumble, and the characteristic packed effects are apt to degenerate into cluttered obscurity.

The development, however, it seems reasonable to suppose, was inevitable. A poet serious enough to impose his pastoral world on us at all could hardly rest in it. Indeed, it was interesting very largely for the same reasons that his tenure of it was precarious. The achievement in any case is a very limited one, but a limited achievement of that kind is notable to-day. Mr Blunden's best poetry, with its simple movements, its conventional decorum, and its frank literary quality, is the poetry of simple pieties (even if the undertones that accompany the use-hallowed mannerisms and the weathered gravity are not so simple). He was able to be, to some purpose, conservative in technique, and to draw upon the eighteenth century, because the immemorial rural order that is doomed was real to him. It is not likely that a serious poet will be traditional in that way again. Mr Blunden is at any rate significant enough to show up the crowd of Georgian pastoralists.

Only a very superficial classification could associate Edward Thomas with Mr Blunden, or with the Georgians at all. He was a very original poet who devoted great technical subtlety to the expression of a distinctively modern sensibility. His art offers an extreme contrast with Mr Blunden's. Mr Blunden's poems are frankly 'composed,' but Edward Thomas's seem to happen. It is only when the complete effect has been registered in the reader's mind that the inevitability and the exquisite economy become apparent. A characteristic poem of his has the air of being a random jotting down of chance impressions and sensations, the record of a moment of relaxed and undirected consciousness. The diction and movement are those of quiet, ruminative speech. But the unobtrusive signs accumulate, and finally one is aware that the outward scene is accessory to an inner theatre. Edward Thomas is concerned with the finer texture of living, the here and now, the ordinary moments, in which for him the 'meaning' (if any) resides. It is as if he were trying to catch some shy intuition on the edge of consciousness that would disappear if looked at directly. Hence, too, the quietness of the movement, the absence of any strong accent or gesture.

October, for instance, opens with the Autumn scene :

The green elm with the one great bough of gold
Lets leaves into the grass slip, one by one,—

> The short hill grass, the mushrooms small milk-
>   white,
> Harebell and scabious and tormentil,
> That blackberry and gorse, in dew and sun,
> Bow down to ; and the wind travels too light
> To shake the fallen birch leaves from the fern ;
> The gossamers wander at their own will.

The exquisite particularity of this distinguishes it
from Georgian ' nature poetry.' But the end of
the poem is not description ; Edward Thomas's
concern with the outer scene is akin to Mrs
Woolf's : unobtrusively the focus shifts [1] and
we become aware of the inner life which the
sensory impressions are notation for.

>   . . . and now I might
> As happy be as earth is beautiful,
> Were I some other or with earth could turn
> In alternation of violet and rose,
> Harebell and snowdrop, at their season due,
> And gorse that has no time not to be gay.
> But if this be not happiness,—who knows ?
> Some day I shall think this a happy day . . .

A whole habit of sensibility is revealed at a
delicate touch.

October illustrates the method ; but to see how
subtly Thomas can use it (it is a method of exploration at the same time as one of expression)
one must go to such a poem as *Old Man*. It starts
with a quiet meditation upon ' Lad's-love or Old

---

[1] I am assuming again that the interested reader will turn up the
poem.

Man,' the ' hoar-green feathery herb almost a tree.' It passes to the child

> Who plucks a feather from the door-side bush
> Whenever she goes in or out of the house.

From the child there is an inevitable transition to the most poignant of realizations :

>   Not a word she says ;
> And I can only wonder how much hereafter
> She will remember, with that bitter scent,
> Of garden rows, and ancient damson trees
> Topping a hedge, a bent path to a door,
> A low thick bush beside the door, and me
> Forbidding her to pick.
>   As for myself,
> Where first I met the bitter scent is lost.
> I, too, often shrivel the grey shreds,
> Sniff them and think and sniff again and try
> Once more to think what it is I am remembering,
> Always in vain.   I cannot like the scent,
> Yet I would rather give up others more sweet,
> With no meaning, than this bitter one.
>
> I have mislaid the key.   I sniff the spray
> And think of nothing ; I see and I hear nothing ;
> Yet seem, too, to be listening, lying in wait
> For what I should, yet never can, remember :
> No garden appears, no path, no hoar-green bush
> Of Lad's-love, or Old Man, no child beside,
> Neither father nor mother, nor any playmate ;
> Only an avenue, dark, nameless, without end.

A phrase in the last passage—' listening, lying in wait for what I should, yet never can, remember ' —describes admirably Thomas's characteristic manner.   The intimations that come, as here, are not of immortality. And it would be difficult to set off Hardy's Victorian solidity better than by contrast with this poem. A far larger proportion of Thomas's work is good than of Hardy's (indeed, the greater part of the collected poems is good), but, on the other hand, one cannot say 'great' confidently of anything of Thomas's, as one can of Hardy's best. The very fidelity with which Thomas records the modern disintegration, the sense of directionlessness

 —How dreary-swift, with naught to travel to,
  Is Time—[1]

implies limitations. But Thomas's negativeness has nothing in common with the vacuity of the Georgians. He was exquisitely sincere and sensitive, and he succeeded in expressing in poetry a representative modern sensibility. It was an achievement of a very rare order, and he has not yet had the recognition he deserves.

Edward Thomas died in the war. The war, besides killing poets, was supposed at the time to have occasioned a great deal of poetry; but the names of very few 'war-poets' are still remembered. Among them the most current (if we exclude Brooke's) is Siegfried Sassoon's. But though his verse made a wholesome immediate impact it hardly calls for much attention here. Wilfrid Owen was really a remarkable poet, and

[1] *The Glory.* (*Collected Poems.*)

his verse is technically interesting. His reputation is becoming well established. Isaac Rosenberg was equally remarkable, and even more interesting technically, and he is hardly known. But Edward Thomas, Owen and Rosenberg together, even if they had been properly recognized at once, could hardly have constituted a challenge to the ruling poetic fashions.

The opposition to the Georgians was already at the time in question (just after the war) Sitwellism. But the Sitwells belong to the history of publicity rather than of poetry. 'Imagism,' indeed, had been initiated before the war. One cannot say, of course, what part it may have played in the development of poets who are now important, but in itself it amounted to little more than a recognition that something was wrong with poetry.[1]

The debilitated nineteenth-century tradition, then, continued without serious challenge, and there had been nothing to suggest seriously a new start.

---

[1] 'I desired to see English become at once more colloquial and more exact, verse more fluid and more exacting of its practitioners, and above all, as I have said, that it should be realized that poetry, as it were dynamically, is a matter of rendering, not comment. You must not say: " I am so happy " ; you must behave as if you were happy. . . .'—*Imagist Anthology*, 1930, Ford Madox Ford, pp. xiii-xiv. ' It legitimatized free verse, cleared the air of musty artifice and shallow sentiment, revived the clarity and conciseness of the Greeks, substituted classical objectivity for romantic cosmicism, demonstrated the effectiveness of the Oriental miniature, and accomplished a rewedding of the intellect and the emotions.'—*Ibid.*, Glenn Hughes, p. xvii.

At this point it becomes necessary to mention a name that has been left out of the foregoing account—that of Bridges. It is not altogether an accident that no occasion should have presented itself of mentioning him before. If one does not care for him one may say that he is so academic that there is no reason why he should come anywhere in particular. If one feels respectful one may compare him to Landor and say that he is aloof. As for *The Testament of Beauty*, it had not come out at the time in question. That, however, is perhaps not excuse enough for shirking comment. I will say, then, that the description of it quoted from Mr Squire in my introductory chapter seems to me fair. Bridges spent upon this crowning work of his life the profit of a life of technical experimenting, but his kind of interest in technique was not a kind that can concern us much in this study. In *The Testament of Beauty* the technique and the matter are, as it were, parallel interests, having no essential relation with each other. The book is a disquisition in verse that is scholarly and original, but dead. Whatever the commercial success of *The Testament of Beauty* may prove, it is not the existence of a keen and discriminating public for poetry.

III

T. S. Eliot

THE situation upon which Mr Eliot impinged has now been fairly described. The magnitude of the impact may be said to have been registered with the publication of *Poems* 1909-1925 ; but the contents of that volume had appeared at various times earlier. *Prufrock*, the earliest section, which is dated 1917, itself constitutes an important event in the history of English poetry. The title poem, *The Love Song of J. Alfred Prufrock*, which is printed at the beginning of *Poems* 1909-1925, represents a complete break with the nineteenth-century tradition, and a new start. It must indeed have been difficult to take seriously in 1917, for it defies the traditional canon of seriousness :

> I grow old . . . I grow old . . .
> I shall wear the bottoms of my trousers rolled.

Can this be poetry ? And yet there are passages that, for all their oddness of imagery and tone, do not immediately condemn themselves as ' unpoetical ' even by anthological standards :

> The yellow fog that rubs its back upon the window-
> panes,

The yellow smoke that rubs its muzzle on the
    window-panes
Licked its tongue into the corners of the evening,
Lingered upon the pools that stand in drains,
Let fall upon its back the soot that falls from
    chimneys,
Slipped by the terrace, made a sudden leap,
And seeing it was a soft October night,
Curled once about the house, and fell asleep.

—Indeed, it is as necessary to revise the traditional
idea of the distinction between seriousness and
levity in approaching this poetry as in approaching the Metaphysical poetry of the seventeenth
century.   And as striking as this subtlety and
flexibility of tone, this complexity of attitude, is
the nature (exemplified in the passage just quoted)
of the imagery.   The canons of the poetical are
forgotten ; the poet assumes the right to make
use of any materials that seem to him significant.
We have here, in short, poetry that expresses
freely a modern sensibility, the ways of feeling,
the modes of experience, of one fully alive in his
own age.   Already the technical achievement is
such as to be rich in promise of development and
application.

   Yet it must be admitted that if *The Love Song of
J. Alfred Prufrock* stood alone there would be
some excuse for unreadiness to recognize in it this
kind of significance.   A certain heaviness about
the gestures (' heavy ' in the sense of caricature)—

> Do I dare
> Disturb the universe?

and

> Though I have seen my head (grown slightly bald)
>   brought in upon a platter

—emphasizes the touch of conscious elegance in the disillusion, and makes ' clever ' seem a more adequate description than it ought :

> I have seen the moment of my greatness flicker,
> And I have seen the eternal Footman hold my coat,
>   and snicker,
> And in short, I was afraid.

But in *Portrait of a Lady* the poise is more subtle, and it is maintained with sure and exquisite delicacy. The poet's command both of his experience and of his technique (if we can distinguish) is perfect. Without any limiting suggestion of caricature he can write :

> And I must borrow every changing shape
> To find expression . . . dance, dance
> Like a dancing bear,
> Cry like a parrot, chatter like an ape.
> Let us take the air, in a tobacco trance—
> Well! and what if she should die some afternoon,
> Afternoon grey and smoky, evening yellow and
>   rose;
> Should die and leave me sitting pen in hand
> With the smoke coming down above the house-
>   tops . . .

The flexibility and the control of this are main-

tained throughout the poem. The utterances of
the lady are in the idiom and cadence of modern
speech, and they go perfectly with the movement
of the verse, which, for all its freedom and variety,
is nevertheless very strict and precise. The poet is
as close to the contemporary world as any novelist
could be, and his formal verse medium makes
possible a concentration and a directness, audacities of transition and psychological notation, such
as are forbidden to the novelist. Only a very
strong originality could so have triumphed over
traditional habits, and only very strong preconceptions could hinder the poem's being recognized as the work of a major poet.

Portrait of a Lady is the most remarkable thing
in the *Prufrock* section. *Preludes* and *Rhapsody on
a Windy Night* develop that imagery of urban
disillusion which has since done so much service
in the verse of adolescent romantic pessimists.
The use of this imagery relates him to Baudelaire,
and the occasion now arises to note his debt to
certain later French poets. To a young practitioner faced with Mr Eliot's problems Tristan
Corbière and Jules Laforgue offered starting
points such as were not to be found in English
poetry of the nineteenth century. How closely he
studied French verse may be gathered from the
verse, retained in *Poems* 1909-1925, that he himself wrote in French. He learnt, by his own

account, from Jules Laforgue in particular, and the evidence is apparent in his early work. The evidence lies not so much in a Laforguian exercise like *Conversation Galante* as in *The Love Song of J. Alfred Prufrock* and *Portrait of a Lady*. It is difficult to distinguish between attitude and technique : he was able to derive means of expression from Laforgue because of a certain community with him in situation and sensibility. The self-ironical, self-distrustful attitudes of *Prufrock* owe their definition largely to Laforgue, and there the technical debt shows itself ; it shows itself in the ironical transitions, and also in the handling of the verse. But this last head has been made too much of by some critics : French moves so differently from English that to learn from French verse an English poet must be strongly original. And to learn as Mr Eliot learnt in general from Laforgue is to be original to the point of genius. Already in the collection of 1917 he is himself as only a major poet can be.

The other derivation he assigns to his verse—' the form in which I began to write, in 1908 or 1909, was directly drawn from the study of Laforgue together with the later Elizabethan drama'[1]—manifests itself plainly in the first poem of the section following *Prufrock*, that dated 1920. It is not for nothing that in *Geron-*

[1] *Selected Poems of Ezra Pound : Introduction*, p. viii.

tion he alludes to one of the finest passages of
Middleton :

> I that was near your heart was removed there-
> from
> To lose beauty in terror, terror in inquisition.
> I have lost my passion : why should I need to
> keep it
> Since what is kept must be adulterated ?
> *Gerontion.*

> I that am of your blood was taken from you
> For your better health ; look no more upon it,
> But cast it to the ground regardlessly.
> Let the common sewer take it from distinction.
> *The Changeling*, v. iii.

The comparison would be worth making at
greater length in order to bring out, not only the
likeness in movement of Mr Eliot's verse to
mature Elizabethan dramatic verse, but also
Mr Eliot's astonishing power. Nowhere in
Middleton, or, for that matter, Webster, Tourneur, or anywhere outside Shakespeare, can we
find a passage so sustained in quality as *Gerontion*.
In his essay on Massinger [1] he says : ' with the
end of Chapman, Middleton, Webster, Tourneur,
Donne we end a period when the intellect was
immediately at the tips of the senses. Sensation
became word and word sensation.' *Gerontion*
answers to this description as well as anything by
any of the authors enumerated : it expresses psy-

---

[1] *The Sacred Wood*, p. 117.

chological subtleties and complexities in imagery of varied richness and marvellously sure realization. The whole body of the words seems to be used. Qualities that (if we ignore Hopkins as he was ignored) have been absent from English poetry since the period that Mr Eliot describes (his critical preoccupation with it is significant) reappear with him.

The effect of his few and brief critical references to Milton is notorious. The effect upon Miltonic influence of his practice is likely to be even more radical. If we look at the first *Hyperion* of Keats we see that it points forward to Tennyson and backward to Milton. This simple reminder (a safe generalization would call for more qualifying than is in place here) serves to bring home the prevalence of certain limitations in the way in which English has been used in poetry since Milton. Milton and Tennyson are very different, but when Tennyson, or any other poet of the nineteenth century (which saw a rough first draft in the revised *Hyperion*), wrote blank verse, even when he intended it to be dramatic, it followed Milton rather than Shakespeare—a Milton who could be associated with Spenser. Even when Shakespeare was consciously the model, it was a Shakespeare felt through Milton. Language was used in a generally Miltonic way even in un-Miltonic verse. To justify the phrase, ' a generally Miltonic way,' a difficult and varying analysis would be necessary; but I have in mind Milton's habit of exploiting language as a kind of musical medium outside himself, as it were. There is no pressure in his verse of any complex and varying current of feeling and sensation; the words have little substance or muscular quality: Milton is using only a small part of the resources of the English language. The remoteness of his poetic idiom from his own speech is to be considered here. ('English must be kept up,' said Keats, explaining his abandonment of the Miltonic first *Hyperion*). A man's most vivid emotional and sensuous experience is inevitably bound up with the language that he actually speaks.

The brief account given above of the relation of *Gerontion* to Middleton and his contemporaries must not be allowed to suggest that Mr Eliot's verse has anything in it of pastiche. For all its richness and variety and power of assimilating odds and ends from Lancelot Andrewes (for instance), its staple idiom and movement derive immediately from modern speech.

These considerations have been put too briefly to be critically impregnable: no simple formula will cover poetic practice in the nineteenth century. That they can be put so briefly and yet serve their purpose, that one can take so much for understood, is due to Mr Eliot. That young practitioners are now using words very differently from the poets of the last age is also due mainly to him.

The dramatic derivation of the verse is not all that there is dramatic about *Gerontion* : it has a really dramatic detachment. In this respect it represents a great advance upon anything printed earlier in *Poems* 1909-1925. *Prufrock* and *Portrait of a Lady* are concerned with the directly personal embarrassments, disillusions and distresses of a sophisticated young man. It is not a superficial difference that *Gerontion* has for *persona* an old man, embodying a situation remote from that of the poet. From a position far above his immediate concerns as a particular individual, projecting himself, as it were, into a comprehensive and representative human consciousness, the poet contemplates human life and asks what it all comes to. The introductory quotation gives the hint :

> *Thou hast nor youth nor age*
> *But as it were an after dinner sleep*
> *Dreaming of both.*

—*Gerontion* has the impersonality of great poetry.

In method, too, *Gerontion* represents a development. Since the method is that, or a large part of that, of *The Waste Land*, it seems better to risk some elementary observations upon it, for *The Waste Land* has been found difficult. Instructions

how to read the poem (should anything more than
the title and the epigraph be necessary) are given
in the last line :

> Tenants of the house,
> Thoughts of a dry brain in a dry season.

It has neither narrative nor logical continuity, and
the only theatre in which the characters mentioned
come together, or could, is the mind of the old
man. The Jew who squats on the window-sill
could not hear the old man even if he spoke his
thoughts aloud, and the field overhead in which
the goat coughs has no geographical relation to
the house. All the persons, incidents and images
are there to evoke the immediate consciousness of
the old man as he broods over a life lived through
and asks what is the outcome, what the meaning,
what the residue. This seems simple enough, and
the transitions and associations are not obscure.

The poem opens with what is to be a recurrent
theme of Mr Eliot's : the mixing of ' memory and
desire ' in present barrenness. The old man in
his ' dry month,' waiting for the life-giving ' rain '
that he knows will never come, is stirred to envy,
then to poignant recollection, by the story of
hot-blooded vitality, which contrasts with the
squalor of his actual surroundings. Youthful
desire mingles in memory with the most exalted
emotions, those associated with the mysteries of
religion :

The word within a word, unable to speak a word,
Swaddled with darkness.   In the juvescence of the
    year
Came Christ the tiger.

In depraved May . . .

Here, in the last two phrases, Mr Eliot does in
concentration what he does by his notorious
transitions from theme to theme : widely different
emotions and feelings are contrasted and fused.
It is the kind of effect that Shakespeare gets in
such a line as

Lilies that fester smell far worse than weeds,[1]

where the associations that cluster round ' lilies '
—fragrant flowers and emblems of purity—are
contrasted and fused with those attaching to
' fester,' which applies to rotting flesh.

In *Gerontion* the contrast is developed : the
emotional intensities evoked by the reference to
the Sacrament are contrasted with the stale cosmopolitan depravity evoked by the names and by
the suggested incidents and associations :

To be eaten, to be divided, to be drunk
Among whispers ; by Mr Silvero
With caressing hands, at Limoges
Who walked all night in the next room ;

By Hakagawa, bowing among the Titians ;
By Madame de Tornquist, in the dark room
Shifting the candles ; Fräulein von Kulp
Who turned in the hall, one hand on the door.

[1] Sonnet 94.

' Among whispers ' may be pointed to as a characteristic transition. They are first the whispers of religious awe ; then, in the new context, they become clandestine and sinister, the whispers of intrigue. The reference to ' the Titians ' brings in art : art and religion, the two refuges from time and the sordid actuality, suffer the same staling depravation. Fräulein von Kulp is seen vividly, a precise particular figure in a precise particular posture, but far in the past ; she serves only to emphasize the present vacancy :

> Vacant shuttles
> Weave the wind.   I have no ghosts,
> An old man in a draughty house
> Under a windy knob.

But this kind of elucidation is perhaps insulting. At any rate, no more can be needed : more than enough has been done to illustrate the method. And only an analysis on Mr Empson's lines [1] could be anything like fair to the subtleties of the poem ; for Mr Eliot's effects depend a great deal upon ambiguity. One of the most obvious instances occurs near the end :

> . . . De Bailhache, Fresca, Mrs Cammel, whirled
> Beyond the circuit of the shuddering Bear
> In fractured atoms.   Gull against the wind, in the
>   windy straits
> Of Belle Isle, or running on the Horn,
> White feathers in the snow, the Gulf claims,

[1] See *Seven Types of Ambiguity*, W. Empson (Chatto and Windus).

And an old man driven by the Trades
To a sleepy corner.

The gull following upon those names that evoke
The News of the World enforces partly the inevitable end, the common reduction to 'fractured
atoms.' A bunch of feathers blown in the gale,
it brings home poignantly the puny helplessness
of the individual life. But also, in its clean, swift
vitality, it contrasts with the frowsy squalor of
finance, crime and divorce. Similarly with respect to the old man: it stands to him for inevitable death and dissolution; but it also stands for
the strength and ardour that he has lost.

There would seem to be little to impede the
recognition of *Gerontion* as great poetry. But
Burbank with a Baedeker : Bleistein with a Cigar and
certain other of the poems that follow develop
(giving definition at the same time to a characteristic preoccupation of the poet) a technical device
that seems to have been responsible for some of
the recalcitrance shown towards *The Waste Land*.
They use as essential means quotation and allusion.
The references in *Burbank* to *Antony and Cleopatra*
are obvious, and their purpose is plainly a kind of
ironical contrast: heroic love, lust in the grand
style and the pitiful modern instance. The
characteristic preoccupation which I have mentioned some critics see as a tendency to condemn
the present by the standards of an ideal past.

This is too simple an account. In *Sweeney Among the Nightingales*, for example, the contrast is clearly something more than that between the sordid incident in a modern brothel and the murder of Agamemnon :

> The circles of the stormy moon
> Slide westward towards the River Plate,
> Death and the Raven drift above
> And Sweeney guards the horned gate.
>
> Gloomy Orion and the Dog
> Are veiled ; and hushed the shrunken seas ;
> The person in the Spanish cape
> Tries to sit on Sweeney's knees,
>
> Slips and pulls the table cloth
> Overturns a coffee-cup

     .   .   .   .

Moreover, the number of allusions in *Burbank* has not yet been taken account of. There is no need to enumerate them : they refer to half-a-dozen or more authors. The best commentary on them, perhaps, is *A Cooking Egg*, which does not represent Mr Eliot at his best, but exhibits his *procédé* with especial plainness. It is not merely as foils to the mean actuality that these varied references are there. The wide culture, the familiarity with various cultures, that they represent has a closer bearing upon the sense of stale disillusion. This point will be made clear when we come to *The Waste Land*.

I have been a good deal embarrassed by the

fear of dwelling on the obvious to the extent of
insulting the reader. But where Mr Eliot's poetry
is concerned it still seems necessary to say elementary things. It is still possible for a critic
belonging to a younger generation than Mr
Eliot's to remark of one of those ironical contrasts that we have been considering :

> In regard to the pretty-pretty element, it seems
> evident that the names Nausicaa and Polypheme,
> while not to be regarded merely as pretty-pretty
> (because the poem contains sordid phrases too), are,
> to a certain extent, conversely, to be looked on as
> jam to help us take the bitter sordid powder.[1]

The essay to which this is a footnote appears in
the second volume of *Scrutinies*, and itself deserves
a brief scrutiny, since that volume makes some
pretension to represent the young advance-guard
of criticism, and the essayist is in intelligent
company. The misgiving aroused by the title—
The Lyric Impulse in the Poetry of T. S. Eliot—finds
unexpectedly thorough confirmation. Mr Eliot's
'lyric impulse,' we discover, is 'his poetic,
Shelleyan impulse.' When, in spite of his resist-
ant sophistication, he yields to it he breaks into
' pure English lyric style.' The third part of *The
Waste Land* is judged to be more unified than the
rest ' perhaps because the subject, sensual love, is
naturally more close to Mr Eliot's heart (as to the
heart of a lyric poet) than the more abstract con-

[1] *Scrutinies*, ii. Collected by Edgell Rickword, p. 16.

siderations with which the other parts of the poem wish to deal. . . .' We find propounded as a theme for critical treatment 'the poetisation of the unpoetical.' In short, what the critic, in the latest idiom and accent, is applying to the diagnosis of Mr Eliot is the familiar idea of the intrinsically poetical.

Some elementary observation, then, is not unwarranted. And, immediately, it may be noted that this testimony to the strength of the 'poetical' tradition brings out the greatness of Mr Eliot's achievement: in his work by 1920 English poetry had made a new start.

It was *The Waste Land* that compelled recognition for the achievement. The poem appeared first in the opening numbers of *The Criterion* (October 1922 and January 1923). The title, we know, comes from Miss J. L. Weston's book, *From Ritual to Romance*, the theme of which is anthropological: the Waste Land there has a significance in terms of Fertility Ritual. What is the significance of the modern Waste Land ? The answer may be read in what appears as the rich disorganization of the poem. The seeming disjointedness is intimately related to the erudition that has annoyed so many readers [1] and to the

---

[1] 'I don't like his erudition-traps,' said a very distinguished author to me once. And this, from *Gallion's Reach* (pp. 35-36), by H. M. Tomlinson, is representative:

'His grin broadened. "All I can say is, my dear, give me the old

wealth of literary borrowings and allusions. These characteristics reflect the present state of civilization. The traditions and cultures have mingled, and the historical imagination makes the past contemporary ; no one tradition can digest so great a variety of materials, and the result is a break-down of forms and the irrevocable loss of that sense of absoluteness which seems necessary to a robust culture. The bearing of this on the technique developed in *Burbank* and *A Cooking Egg* does not need enlarging upon.

In considering our present plight we have also to take account of the incessant rapid change that characterizes the Machine Age. The result is breach of continuity and the uprooting of life. This last metaphor has a peculiar aptness, for what we are witnessing to-day is the final uprooting of the immemorial ways of life, of life rooted in the soil. The urban imagery that affiliates

---

songs, though I can't sing them, if they're the new. What does poetry want with footnotes about psycho-analysis and negro mythology ? "

' " Suppose," someone asked him, " that you don't know anything about them ? "

' " Well, I couldn't get them out of footnotes and the poetry all at one stride, could I ? But Doris, they were very clever and insulting poems, I think. Sing a song of mockery. Is that the latest ? But it was a surprising little book, though it smelt like the dissection of bad innards." '

The novelist, with a certain subtle naïveté, clearly identifies himself with the attitude, and he clearly means the reader to do the same. And there is every reason to suppose that he would not object to the reader's supposing that he had Mr Eliot in mind. The First Edition of *Gallion's Reach* is valuable.

Mr Eliot to Baudelaire and Laforgue has its significance; a significance that we touched on in glancing at the extreme contrast between Mr Eliot and Hardy. We may take Mr T. F. Powys to-day as the successor of Hardy: he is probably the last considerable artist of the old order (he seems to me a great one). It does not seem likely that it will ever again be possible for a distinguished mind to be formed, as Mr Powys has been, on the rhythms, sanctioned by nature and time, of rural culture. The spirit of *Mr Weston's Good Wine* could not be described as one of traditional faith; all the more striking, then, is the contrast in effect between Mr Powys's and Mr Eliot's preoccupation with ' birth, copulation and death.' [1] Mr Powys's disillusion belongs to the old world, and the structure and organization of his art are according. There is no need to elaborate the comparison.

The remoteness of the civilization celebrated in *The Waste Land* from the natural rhythms is brought out, in ironical contrast, by the anthropo-

[1]   '. . .
           Nothing at all but three things
DORIS.   What things?
SWEENEY.   Birth, copulation, and death.
           That's all, that's all, that's all, that's all.
           Birth, copulation, and death.
DORIS.   I'd be bored
SWEENEY.   You'd be bored.
           Birth, copulation, and death.'
                Fragment of an Agon. Criterion, Jan. 1927.

logical theme. Vegetation cults, fertility ritual, with their sympathetic magic, represent a harmony of human culture with the natural environment, and express an extreme sense of the unity of life. In the modern Waste Land

> April is the cruellest month, breeding
> Lilacs out of the dead land,

but bringing no quickening to the human spirit. Sex here is sterile, breeding not life and fulfilment but disgust, accidia and unanswerable questions. It is not easy to-day to accept the perpetuation and multiplication of life as ultimate ends.

But the anthropological background has positive functions. It plays an obvious part in evoking that particular sense of the unity of life which is essential to the poem. It helps to establish the level of experience at which the poem works, the mode of consciousness to which it belongs. In *The Waste Land* the development of impersonality that *Gerontion* shows in comparison with *Prufrock* reaches an extreme limit : it would be difficult to imagine a completer transcendence of the individual self, a completer projection of awareness. We have, in the introductory chapter, considered the poet as being at the conscious point of his age. There are ways in which it is possible to be too conscious ; and to be so is, as a result of the break-up of forms and the loss of axioms noted

above, one of the troubles of the present age (if
the abstraction may be permitted, consciousness
being in any case a minority affair). We recognize
in modern literature the accompanying sense of
futility.

The part that science in general has played in
the process of disintegration is matter of common-
place : anthropology is, in the present context, a
peculiarly significant expression of the scientific
spirit.   To the anthropological eye beliefs,
religions and moralities are human habits—in
their odd variety too human. Where the anthropological outlook prevails, sanctions wither.
In a contemporary consciousness there is inevitably a great deal of the anthropological, and the
background of *The Waste Land* is thus seen to
have a further significance.

To be, then, too much conscious and conscious
of too much—that is the plight :

>   After such knowledge, what forgivenness ?

At this point Mr Eliot's note [1] on Tiresias deserves attention :

>   Tiresias, although a mere spectator and not
> indeed a ' character,' is yet the most important
> personage in the poem, uniting all the rest.   Just as
> the one-eyed merchant, seller of currants, melts into
> the Phoenician Sailor, and the latter is not wholly
> distinct from Ferdinand Prince of Naples, so all the

---

[1] Note to line 218 of *The Waste Land* (*Poems* 1909-1925, p. 88).

women are one woman, and the two sexes meet in Tiresias. What Tiresias *sees*, in fact, is the substance of the poem.

If Mr Eliot's readers have a right to a grievance, is it that he has not given this note more salience ; for it provides the clue to *The Waste Land*. It indicates plainly enough what the poem is : an effort to focus an inclusive human consciousness. The effort, in ways suggested above, is characteristic of the age ; and in an age of psycho-analysis, an age that has produced the last section of *Ulysses*, Tiresias—' venus huic erat utraque nota ' —presents himself as the appropriate impersonation. A cultivated modern is (or feels himself to be) intimately aware of the experience of the opposite sex.

Such an undertaking offers a difficult problem of organization, a distinguishing character of the mode of consciousness that promotes it being a lack of organizing principle, the absence of any inherent direction. A poem that is to contain all myths cannot construct itself upon one. It is here that *From Ritual to Romance* comes in. It provides a background of reference that makes possible something in the nature of a musical [1] organization. Let us start by considering the use of the Tarot pack. Introduced in the first section,

[1] Mr I. A. Richards uses the analogy from music in some valuable notes on Mr Eliot that are printed in an appendix to the later editions of *The Principles of Literary Criticism*.

suggesting, as it does, destiny, chance and the
eternal mysteries, it at once intimates the scope
of the poem, the mode of its contemplation of
life. It informs us as to the nature of the characters : we know that they are such as could not
have relations with one another in any narrative
scheme, and could not be brought together on
any stage, no matter what liberties were taken
with the Unities. The immediate function of the
passage introducing the pack, moreover, is to
evoke, in contrast with what has preceded,
cosmopolitan ' high life,' and the charlatanism
that battens upon it :

> Madame Sosostris, famous clairvoyante,
> Had a bad cold, nevertheless
> Is known to be the wisest woman in Europe,
> With a wicked pack of cards.

Mr Eliot can achieve the banality appropriate
here, and achieve at the same time, when he wants
it, a deep undertone, a resonance, as it were, of
fate :

>   . . . and this card,
> Which is blank, is something he carries on his back,
> Which I am forbidden to see.   I do not find
> The Hanged Man.   Fear death by water.
> I see crowds of people, walking round in a ring.

The peculiar menacing undertone of this associates
it with a passage in the fifth section :

> Who is the third who walks always beside you ?
> When I count, there are only you and I together

But when I look ahead up the white road
There is always another one walking beside you
Gliding wrapt in a brown mantle, hooded
I do not know whether a man or a woman
—But who is that on the other side of you?

The association establishes itself without any help
from Mr Eliot's note; it is there in any case, as
any fit reader of poetry can report; but the note
helps us to recognize its significance:

> The Hanged Man, a member of the traditional
> pack, fits my purpose in two ways: because he is
> associated in my mind with the Hanged God of
> Frazer, and because I associate him with the
> hooded figure in the passage of the disciples to
> Emmaus in Part V.

The Tarot pack, Miss Weston has established,
has affiliations with fertility ritual, and so lends
itself peculiarly to Mr Eliot's purpose: the
instance before us illustrates admirably how he
has used its possibilities. The hooded figure in
the passage just quoted is Jesus. Perhaps our
being able to say so depends rather too much
upon Mr Eliot's note; but the effect of the
passage does not depend so much upon the note
as might appear. For Christ has figured already
in the opening of the section (see *What the
Thunder Said*):

> After the torchlight red on sweaty faces
> After the frosty silence in the gardens
> After the agony in stony places

> The shouting and the crying
> Prison and palace and reverberation
> Of thunder of spring over distant mountains
> He who was living is now dead
> We who were living are now dying
> With a little patience

The reference is unmistakable. Yet it is not only
Christ ; it is also the Hanged God and all the
sacrificed gods : with the ' thunder of spring '
' Adonis, Attis, Osiris ' and all the others of *The
Golden Bough* come in. And the ' agony in stony
places ' is not merely the Agony in the Garden ;
it is also the agony of the Waste Land, introduced
in the first section : (*The Burial of the Dead*,
ll. 19 ff.).

> What are the roots that clutch, what branches
>   grow
> Out of this stony rubbish ?   Son of man,
> You cannot say, or guess, for you know only
> A heap of broken images, where the sun beats,
> And the dead tree gives no shelter, the cricket
>   no relief,
> And the dry stone no sound of water.

In *What the Thunder Said* the drouth becomes
(among other things) a thirst for the waters of
faith and healing, and the specifically religious
enters into the orchestration of the poem. But
the thunder is ' dry sterile thunder without rain ' ;
there is no resurrection or renewal ; and after the
opening passage the verse loses all buoyancy, and

takes on a dragging, persistent movement as of hopeless exhaustion—

> Here is no water but only rock
> Rock and no water and the sandy road
> The road winding above among the mountains
> Which are mountains of rock without water

—the imagined sound of water coming in as a torment. There is a suggestion of fever here, a sultry ominousness—

> There is not even solitude in the mountains

—and it is this which provides the transition to the passage about the hooded figure quoted above. The ominous tone of this last passage associates it, as we have seen, with the reference (ll. 55-56) to the Hanged Man in the Tarot passage of *The Burial of the Dead*. So Christ becomes the Hanged Man, the Vegetation God ; and at the same time the journey through the Waste Land along ' the sandy road' becomes the Journey to Emmaus. Mr Eliot gives us a note on the ' third who walks always beside you ' :

> The following lines were stimulated by the account of one of the Antarctic expeditions (I forget which, but I think one of Shackleton's) : it was related that the party of explorers, at the extremity of their strength, had the constant delusion that there was *one more member* than could actually be counted.

This might be taken to be, from our point of view, merely an interesting irrelevance, and it certainly is not necessary. But it nevertheless serves to intimate the degree of generality that Mr Eliot intends to accompany his concrete precision : he is both definite and vague at once. ' Just as the one-eyed merchant, seller of currants, melts into the Phoenician Sailor, and the latter is not wholly distinct from Ferdinand Prince of Naples '—so one experience is not wholly distinct from another experience of the same general order ; and just as all experiences ' meet in Tiresias,' so a multitude of experiences meet in each passage of the poem. Thus the passage immediately in question has still further associations. That same hallucinatory quality which relates it to what goes before recalls also the neurasthenic episode (ll. 111 ff.) in *A Game of Chess* (the second section) :

> ' What is that noise ? '
>> The wind under the door.
> ' What is that noise now ? . . .'

All this illustrates the method of the poem, and the concentration, the depth of orchestration that Mr Eliot achieves ; the way in which the themes move in and out of one another and the predominance shifts from level to level. The transition from this passage is again by way of the general ominousness, which passes into hallucinated vision and then into nightmare :

—But who is that on the other side of you ?

What is that sound high in the air
Murmur of maternal lamentation
Who are those hooded hordes swarming
Over endless plains, stumbling in cracked earth
Ringed by the flat horizon only
What is the city over the mountains
Cracks and reforms and bursts in the violet air
Falling towers
Jerusalem Athens Alexandria
Vienna London
Unreal.

The focus of attention shifts here to the outer disintegration in its large, obvious aspects, and the references to Russia and to post-war Europe in general are plain. The link between the hooded figure of the road to Emmaus and the ' hooded hordes swarming ' is not much more than verbal (though appropriate to a fevered consciousness), but this phrase has an essential association with a line (56) in the passage that introduces the Tarot pack :

I see crowds of people, walking round in a ring.

These ' hooded hordes,' ' ringed by the flat horizon only,' are not merely Russians, suggestively related to the barbarian invaders of civilization ; they are also humanity walking endlessly round in a ring, a further illustration of the eternal futility. ' Unreal ' picks up the ' Unreal city ' of *The Burial of the Dead* (l. 60), where ' Saint

Mary Woolnoth kept the hours,' and the unreality
gets further development in the nightmare passage
that follows :

> And upside down in air were towers
> Tolling reminiscent bells, that kept the hours
> And voices singing out of empty cisterns and
>   exhausted wells.

Then, with a transitional reference (which will
be commented on later) to the theme of the
Chapel Perilous, the focus shifts inwards again.
'Datta,' 'dayadhvam,' and 'damyata,' the ad-
monitions of the thunder, are explained in a note,
and in this case, at any rate, the reliance upon the
note justifies itself. We need only be told once
that they mean 'give, sympathize, control,' and
the context preserves the meaning. The Sanscrit
lends an appropriate portentousness, intimating
that this is the sum of wisdom according to a
great tradition, and that what we have here is a
radical scrutiny into the profit of life. The irony,
too, is radical :

> *Datta* : what have we given ?
> My friend, blood shaking my heart
> The awful daring of a moment's surrender
> Which an age of prudence can never retract
> By this, and this only, we have existed
>   .   .   .   .   .

—it is an equivocal comment. And for comment
on 'sympathize' we have a reminder of the
irremediable isolation of the individual. After all

the agony of sympathetic transcendence, it is to
the individual, the focus of consciousness, that
we return :

> Shall I at least set my lands in order?

The answer comes in the bundle of fragments
that ends the poem, and, in a sense, sums it up.

Not that the *poem* lacks organization and unity.
The frequent judgments that it does betray a
wrong approach.   The author of *The Lyric
Impulse in the Poetry of T. S. Eliot*, for instance,
speaks of ' a definitely willed attempt to weld
various fine fragments into a metaphysical whole.'
But the unity of *The Waste Land* is no more
' metaphysical ' than it is narrative or dramatic,
and to try to elucidate it metaphysically reveals
complete misunderstanding.   The unity the poem
aims at is that of an inclusive consciousness : the
organization it achieves as a work of art is of the
kind that has been illustrated, an organization
that may, by analogy, be called musical.   It
exhibits no progression :

> I sat upon the shore
> Fishing, with the arid plain behind me

—the thunder brings no rain to revive the Waste
Land, and the poem ends where it began.

At this point the criticism has to be met that,
while all this may be so, the poem in any case
exists, and can exist, only for an extremely limited

public equipped with special knowledge. The
criticism must be admitted. But that the public
for it is limited is one of the symptoms of the
state of culture that produced the poem. Works
expressing the finest consciousness of the age in
which the word 'high-brow' has become current
are almost inevitably such as to appeal only to a
tiny minority.[1] It is still more serious that this
minority should be more and more cut off from
the world around it—should, indeed, be aware of
a hostile and overwhelming environment. This
amounts to an admission that there must be something limited about the kind of artistic achievement possible in our time : even Shakespeare in
such conditions could hardly have been the
'universal' genius. And *The Waste Land*, clearly,
is not of the order of *The Divine Comedy* or of
Lear. The important admission, then, is not that
The Waste Land can be appreciated only by a very
small minority (how large in any age has the
minority been that has really comprehended the
masterpieces ?), but that this limitation carries
with it limitations in self-sufficiency.

These limitations, however, are easily over-
stressed. Most of the 'special knowledge,'
dependence upon which is urged against *The
Waste Land*, can fairly be held to be common to

[1] This matter is discussed at length by the present author in *Mass
Civilisation and Minority Culture* (see *For Continuity*).

the public that would in any case read modern
poetry. The poem does, indeed, to some extent
lean frankly upon *From Ritual to Romance*. And
sometimes it depends upon external support in
ways that can hardly be justified. Let us take,
for instance, the end of the third section, *The
Fire Sermon* :

la la

To Carthage then I came

Burning, burning, burning, burning
O Lord Thou pluckest me out
O Lord Thou pluckest

burning

It is plain from Mr Eliot's note on this passage—
' The collocation of these two representatives of
eastern and western asceticism, as the culmination
of this part of the poem, is not an accident '—that
he intends St Augustine and the Buddha to be
actively present here. But whereas one cursory
reading of *From Ritual to Romance* does all (prac-
tically) that is assigned as function to that book,
no amount of reading of the *Confessions* or
Buddhism in Translation will give these few words
power to evoke the kind of presence of ' eastern
and western asceticism ' that seems necessary to
the poem : they remain, these words, mere
pointers to something outside. We can only
conclude that Mr Eliot here has not done as much

as he supposes. And so with the passage
(ll. 385 ff.) in *What the Thunder Said* bringing in
the theme of the Chapel Perilous : it leaves too
much to Miss Weston ; repeated recourse to
From Ritual to Romance will not invest it with the
virtue it would assume. The irony, too, of the

　　　　　　Shantih　　shantih　　shantih

that ends the poem is largely ineffective, for
Mr Eliot's note that ' " The Peace which passeth
understanding " is a feeble translation of the
content of this word ' can impart to the word
only a feeble ghost of that content for the
Western reader.

Yet the weaknesses of this kind are not nearly
as frequent or as damaging as critics of *The Waste
Land* seem commonly to suppose. It is a self-
subsistent poem, and should be obviously such.
The allusions, references and quotations usually
carry their own power with them as well as being
justified in the appeal they make to special knowledge. 'Unreal City' (l. 60), to take an extreme
instance from one end of the scale, owes nothing
to Baudelaire (whatever Mr Eliot may have
owed) ; the note is merely interesting—though,
of course, it is probable that a reader unacquainted
with Baudelaire will be otherwise unqualified.
The reference to Dante that follows—

A crowd flowed over London Bridge, so many,
I had not thought death had undone so many

—has an independent force, but much is lost to the reader who does not catch the implied comparison between London and Dante's Hell. Yet the requisite knowledge of Dante is a fair demand. The knowledge of *Antony and Cleopatra* assumed in the opening of *A Game of Chess*, or of *The Tempest* in various places elsewhere, no one will boggle at. The main references in *The Waste Land* come within the classes represented by these to Dante and Shakespeare; while of the many others most of the essential carry enough of their power with them. By means of such references and quotations Mr Eliot attains a compression, otherwise unattainable, that is essential to his aim; a compression approaching simultaneity—the co-presence in the mind of a number of different orientations, fundamental attitudes, orders of experience.

This compression and the methods it entails do make the poem difficult reading at first, and a full response comes only with familiarity. Yet the complete rout so often reported, or inadvertently revealed—as, for instance, by the critic who assumes that *The Waste Land* is meant to be a ' metaphysical whole '—can be accounted for only by a wrong approach, an approach with inappropriate expectations. For the general nature and method of the poem should be obvious at first reading. Yet so commonly does the obvious seem to be missed that perhaps a little more elucidation (this time of the opening section) will not be found offensively superfluous. What follows is a brief analysis of *The Burial of the Dead*, the avowed intention being to point out the obvious themes and transitions : anything like a full analysis would occupy many times the space.

The first seven lines introduce the vegetation theme, associating it with the stirring of 'memory and desire.' The transition is simple : ' April,' ' spring,' ' winter,'—then

> Summer surprised us, coming over the Starn-
> bergersee
> With a shower of rain . . .

We seem to be going straight forward, but (as the change of movement intimates) we have modulated into another plane. We are now given a particular ' memory,' and a representative one. It introduces the cosmopolitan note, a note of empty sophistication :

> In the mountains, there you feel free.
> I read, much of the night, and go south in the
> winter.   [Cf. ' Winter kept us warm ']

The next transition is a contrast and a comment, bringing this last passage into relation with the first. April may stir dull roots with spring rain, but

> What are the roots that clutch, what branches grow
> Out of this stony rubbish ?

And there follows an evocation of the Waste Land, with references to *Ezekiel* and *Ecclesiastes*, confirming the tone that intimates that this is an agony of the soul (' Son of man ' relates with the Hanged Man and the Hanged God : with him ' who was living ' and ' is now dead ' at the opening of *What the Thunder Said*). The ' fear '—

I will show you fear in a handful of dust

—recurs, in different modes, in the neurasthenic passage (ll. 111 ff.) of *A Game of Chess*, and in the episode of the hooded figure in *What the Thunder Said*. The fear is partly the fear of death, but still more a nameless, ultimate fear, a horror of the completely negative.

Then comes the verse from *Tristan und Isolde*, offering a positive in contrast—the romantic absolute, love. The ' hyacinth girl,' we may say, represents ' memory and desire ' (the hyacinth, directly evocative like the lilacs bred out of the Waste Land, was also one of the flowers associated with the slain vegetation god), and the ' nothing ' of the Waste Land changes into the ecstasy of passion—a contrast, and something more :

—Yet when we came back, late, from the Hyacinth
    garden,
Your arms full, and your hair wet, I could not
Speak, and my eyes failed, I was neither
Living nor dead, and I knew nothing,
Looking into the heart of light, the silence.

In the Waste Land one is neither living nor dead.
Moreover, the neurasthenic passage referred to
above recalls these lines unmistakably, giving
them a sinister modulation :

> ' Speak to me.   Why do you never speak.   Speak.
>   ' What are you thinking of ?   What thinking ?
>   What ?
> ' I never know what you are thinking.   Think.'
>
>   .   .   .   .
>
>   ' Do
> ' You know nothing ?   Do you see nothing ?   Do
>   you remember
> ' Nothing ? '

The further line from *Tristan und Isolde* ends the
passage of romantic love with romantic desolation.   Madame Sosostris, famous clairvoyante,
follows ; she brings in the demi-monde, so
offering a further contrast—

> Here is Belladonna, the Lady of the Rocks,
> The lady of situations

—and introduces the Tarot pack.   This passage
has already received some comment, and it invites
a great deal more.   The ' lady of situations,' to
make an obvious point, appears in the *Game of
Chess*.   The admonition, ' Fear death by water,'
gets its response in the fourth section, *Death by
Water* : death is inevitable, and the life-giving
water thirsted for (and the water out of which all
life comes) cannot save.   But enough has been
said to indicate the function of the Tarot pack,

the way in which it serves in the organization of the poem.

With the 'Unreal City' the background of urban —of ' megalopolitan '—civilization becomes explicit. The allusion to Dante has already been remarked upon, and so has the way in which Saint Mary Woolnoth is echoed by the ' reminiscent bells ' of *What the Thunder Said*. The portentousness of the ' dead sound on the final stroke of nine ' serves as a transition, and the unreality of the City turns into the intense but meaningless horror, the absurd inconsequence, of a nightmare :

> There I saw one I knew, and stopped him, crying :
> ' Stetson !
> ' You who were with me in the ships at Mylae !
> ' That corpse you planted last year in your garden,
> ' Has it begun to sprout ? Will it bloom this
> year ? . . .'

These last two lines pick up again the opening theme. The corpse acquires a kind of nightmare association with the slain god of *The Golden Bough*, and is at the same time a buried memory. Then, after a reference to Webster (Webster's sepulchral horrors are robust), *The Burial of the Dead* ends with the line in which Baudelaire, having developed the themes of

> La sottise, l'erreur, le péché, la lésine

and finally *L'Ennui*, suddenly turns upon the

reader to remind him that he is something more.

The way in which *The Waste Land* is organized, then, should be obvious even without the aid of notes. And the poet's mastery should be as apparent in the organization as in the parts (where it has been freely acclaimed). The touch with which he manages his difficult transitions, his delicate collocations, is exquisitely sure. His tone, in all its subtle variations, exhibits a perfect control. If there is any instance where this last judgment must be qualified, it is perhaps here (from the first passage of *The Fire Sermon*):

> Sweet Thames, run softly till I end my song,
> Sweet Thames, run softly, for I speak not loud or
>   long.
> But at my back in a cold blast I hear
> The rattle of the bones, and chuckle spread from
>   ear to ear.

These last two lines seem to have too much of the caricature quality of *Prufrock* to be in keeping—for a certain keeping is necessary (and Mr Eliot commonly maintains it) even in contrasts. But even if the comment is just, the occasion for it is a very rare exception.

The Waste Land, then, whatever its difficulty, is, or should be, obviously a poem.[1] It is a self-

---

[1] 'It is a test (a positive test, I do not assert that it is always valid negatively), that genuine poetry can communicate before it is understood.'—T. S. Eliot, *Dante*, p. 16.

subsistent poem.   Indeed, though it would lose
if the notes could be suppressed and forgotten,
yet the more important criticism might be said to
be, not that it depends upon them too much, but
rather that without them, and without the support
of *From Ritual to Romance*, it would not lose more.
It has, that is, certain limitations in any case ;
limitations inherent in the conditions that produced it.   Comprehensiveness, in the very nature
of the undertaking, must be in some sense at the
cost of structure : absence of direction, of organizing principle, in life could hardly be made to
subserve the highest kind of organization in art.

But when all qualifications have been urged,
The Waste Land remains a great positive achievement, and one of the first importance for English
poetry.   In it a mind fully alive in the age compels
a poetic triumph out of the peculiar difficulties
facing a poet in the age.   And in solving his own
problem as a poet Mr Eliot did more than solve
the problem for himself.   Even if *The Waste Land*
had been, as used to be said, a ' dead end ' for
him, it would still have been a new start for
English poetry.

But, of course, to judge it a ' dead end ' was
shallow.   It was to ignore the implications of the
effort that alone could have availed to express
formlessness itself as form.   So complete and
vigorous a statement of the Waste Land could

H

hardly (to risk being both crude and impertinent)
forecast an exhausted, hopeless sojourn there. As
for the nature of the effort, the intimacy with
Dante that the poem betrays has its significance.
There is no great distance in time and no gulf of
any kind between the poet of *The Waste Land* and
the critic who associates [1] himself later with ' a
tendency—discernible even in art—toward a
higher and clearer conception of Reason, and a
more severe and serene control of the emotions
by Reason'; and who writes [2] of Proust ' as a
point of demarcation between a generation for
whom the dissolution of value had in itself a
positive value, and the generation which is beginning to turn its attention to an athleticism, a
training, of the soul as severe and ascetic as the
training of the body of a runner.'

Nevertheless, the poem succeeding *The Waste
Land* in *Poems* 1909-1925, and bringing that collection to a close, gave some plausibility to the
superficial verdict. The epigraph of *The Hollow
Men*—' *Mistah Kurtz—he dead* '—coming from
The Heart of Darkness, suggests a dissolution of
all the sanctions of life ; and the tailing off of the
poem into

> *This is the way the world ends
> Not with a bang but a whimper*

[1] *Criterion*, Jan. 1926, vol. iv., p. 5.
[2] *Ibid.*, Oct. 1926, vol. iv., pp. 752-3.

so completely justifies itself that it does not appear
the audacity it is : ' audacity ' suggests too much
vigour.   The poem develops certain elements of
The Waste Land in a kind of neurasthenic agony.
Yet this evocation of

> Shape without form, shade without colour,
> Paralysed force, gesture without motion

is a marvellous positive achievement, and if we
should be tempted to relate too crudely the ' mind
that created ' with ' the man who suffered ' [1] we
have the various drafts [2] to remind us that it is
after all a poem that we are dealing with.   The
terrible closing section, with its nightmare poise
over the grotesque, is a triumph of aplomb.   The
three middle sections begin that exploration of
' the dreamcrossed twilight ' [3] which (in a different
spirit) is to be pursued in *Ash-Wednesday*.

Between *The Hollow Men* and *Ash-Wednesday*
come three poems published separately in the
Ariel series.   These show a curious change.   We
find in them, instead of the fevered torment of
The Hollow Men, a kind of inert resignation.   The
movements are tired and nerveless ; they suggest
marvellously the failure of rhythm.   If the extreme
agony of consciousness has passed, so has the

---

[1] ' . . . the more perfect the artist, the more completely separate
in him will be the man who suffers and the mind which creates. . . .'
—*The Sacred Wood*, p. 48.

[2] See *The Chapbook*, 1924 (No. 39), and *Criterion*, vol. x., p. 170.

[3] See *Ash-Wednesday*, p. 20.

extraordinary vitality that went with it. But the change has another aspect. These three poems reveal a significant preoccupation; they have a direction, and they all point the same way. *Journey of the Magi* and *A Song for Simeon* deal dramatically with their religious theme, the promise of salvation, but the dramatic form amounts to little more than delicacy in the presentment of intimate personal issues :

> . . . were we led all that way for
> Birth or Death ?   There was a Birth, certainly,
> We had evidence and no doubt.   I had seen birth
>   and death,
> But had thought they were different; this Birth
>   was
> Hard and bitter agony for us, like Death, our death.
> We returned to our places, these Kingdoms,
> But no longer at ease here, in the old dispensation,
> With an alien people clutching their gods.
> I should be glad of another death.

The queer, essential equivocalness of this is the poet's, and the dramatic theme, it becomes clear, is a means to the expression of it. The ambivalence comes out still more strikingly in the end of *A Song for Simeon* :

> I am tired with my own life and the lives of those
>   after me,
> I am dying in my own death and the deaths of those
>   after me.
> Let thy servant depart,
> Having seen thy salvation.

It is something very different from an affirmation
that so transforms the original theme : the air is
' thoroughly small and dry.' [1] And yet there is
something positive present, if only a direction of
feeling and contemplation—something specifically religious. At the end of *Animula*, the third
Ariel poem, the liturgical note characteristic of
Ash-Wednesday appears.

What seemed most to distinguish the first poem
of *Ash-Wednesday*, when, as *Perch' io non spero*, it
appeared in *Commerce*,[2] from the *Ariel* poems was
the rhythm. The rhythm varies within the
sequence from part to part, but it is in general
very much more nerved and positive than that of
the *Ariel* poems. In the comparison it is not
extravagant to speak of it as having certain
qualities of ritual ; it produces in a high degree
the frame-effect, establishing apart from the world
a special order of experience, dedicated to spiritual
exercises. To discuss *Ash-Wednesday*, then, is a
delicate business, incurring danger both of crudity
and impertinence. We remind ourselves of Mr
Eliot's precept and practice in criticism : the
sequence is poetry, and highly formal poetry.
Yet it is impossible not to see in it a process of
self-scrutiny, of self-exploration ; or not to feel
that the poetical problem at any point was a

[1] *Ash-Wednesday*, p. 10.
[2] XV. (Printemps, MCMXXVIII).

spiritual problem, a problem in the attainment of
a difficult sincerity. The poetry belongs to

> . . . the time of tension between dying and birth
> The place of solitude where three dreams cross

and is a striving after a spiritual state based upon
a reality elusive and yet ultimate.

We cannot help recalling Mr Eliot's various
observations about the problem of belief. This,[1]
for instance, seems germane :

> I cannot see that poetry can ever be separated
> from something which I should call belief, and to
> which I cannot see any reason for refusing the name
> of belief, unless we are to reshuffle names together.
> It should hardly be needful to say that it will not
> inevitably be orthodox Christian belief, although
> that possibility can be entertained, since Chris-
> tianity will probably continue to modify itself, as
> in the past, into something that can be believed
> in (I do not mean *conscious* modifications like
> modernism, etc., which always have the op-
> posite effect). The majority of people live below
> the level of belief or doubt. It takes application,
> and a kind of genius, to believe anything, and to
> believe *anything* (I do *not* mean merely to believe in
> some ' religion ') will probably become more and
> more difficult as time goes on.

Mr Eliot's concern is specifically religious. Certain qualities of genius he indubitably has, and
Ash-Wednesday is a disciplined application of them
to the realizing of a spiritual state conceived as

[1] *The Enemy*, Jan. 1927.

depending upon belief—belief in something outside himself. The result is a most subtle poetry
of great technical interest; and it is on the
technical aspect that critical attention must in any
case focus.

For the poet 'technique' was the problem of
sincerity.[1] He had to achieve a paradoxical
precision-in-vagueness; to persuade the elusive
intuition to define itself, without any forcing,
among the equivocations of 'the dreamcrossed
twilight.' The warning against crude interpretation, against trying to elicit anything in the nature
of prose statement, is there in the unexpected
absences of punctuation; and in the repetitive
effects, which suggest a kind of delicate tentative-
ness. The poetry itself is an effort at resolving
diverse impulsions, recognitions and needs.

Ash-Wednesday is a whole. Faced with *Perch'
io non spero* as a separate poem, one might pardon-
ably, perhaps, see an odd affectation in

Why should the agèd eagle stretch its wings ?

But (though the criticism is still made [2]) in a reading of the whole sequence the ironical function of
this self-dramatization becomes obvious. It is an

[1] Cf. 'And this honesty never exists without great technical
accomplishment.'—T. S. Eliot on *Blake* (*The Sacred Wood*, p. 137).

[2] 'And I am made a little tired at hearing Eliot, only in his early
forties, present himself as an "agèd eagle" who asks why he should
make the effort to stretch his wings.'—Edmund Wilson, *Axel's
Castle*, p. 130.

insurance against the pride of humility; a self-admonition against the subtle treasons, the refinements, of egotism that beset the quest of sincerity in these regions. Again,

> And I pray that I may forget
> These matters that with myself I too much discuss
> Too much explain

intimates a capacity for a critical attitude towards the ' discussing ' that the poetry is.

To take fragments separately at their face value is to misunderstand this poetry, which works by compensations, resolutions, residuums and convergences. What, we ask, does the poet resign and renounce in the first poem, and what is the nature of his renunciation? The line from the Shakespeare sonnet suggests that it is worldly ambition, personal glory, that he renounces. This becomes

> The infirm glory of the positive hour;

and

> The one veritable transitory power

together with the next lines—

> Because I cannot drink
> There, where trees flower, and springs flow, for
> there is nothing again

—seems to identify it with the vital illusion of youth. But, it next appears, what we have here is the sensory evocation of a spiritual state:

> Because I know that time is always time
> And place is always and only place
> And what is actual is actual only for one time
> And only for one place
> I rejoice that things are as they are and
> I renounce the blessèd face
> And renounce the voice.

—This, with its bare prose statement, has the effect of a complete renunciation of supernatural assurance. And the general effect of the poem is negative. Yet the formula of renunciation—

> Teach us to care and not to care
> Teach us to sit still

—registers a positive religious impulse, which is confirmed by the liturgical close. And the positive element comes out more significantly in

> Consequently I rejoice, having to construct something
> Upon which to rejoice

—if the air is 'thoroughly small and dry' it is 'smaller and dryer than the will.' Not for nothing have the rhythms of *Ash-Wednesday* so much more life than those of the *Ariel* poems. After this introduction, then, we know what are to be the themes of the following poetry, and what the mode of debate.

It is common to ask of the second poem, 'Who is the Lady, and what do the three white leopards stand for?' As for the first question, Mr Eliot in his *Dante*[1] writes : ' In the Earthly Paradise Dante encounters a lady named Matilda, whose identity need not at first bother us ' ; the identity of the Lady in this poem need not bother us at all. She reminds us not only of Matilda but of Beatrice and Piccarda too, and helps to define a mode of religious contemplation that characterizes the poem. The theme of the poem is death, and death is evoked as complete extinction :

> End of the endless
> Journey to no end
> Conclusion of all that
> Is inconclusible. . .

—But the effect has extraordinarily little in common with that of the same theme in *The Hollow Men* or *Journey of the Magi* or *A Song for Simeon*. The desire for extinction (ἀποθανεῖν θέλω)[2]—

> I should be glad of another death

and

> I am tired with my own life and the lives of those
> after me

—becomes curiously transmuted by association with something positive :

> As I am forgotten
> And would be forgotten, so I would forget
> Thus devoted, concentrated in purpose.

The devotion and the concentration are repre-

---

[1] p. 47.   [2] See the epigraph of *The Waste Land*.

sented by the Lady, who serves to intimate the poet's recourse, in his effort ' to construct something upon which to rejoice,' to a specific religious tradition, and they manifest themselves throughout in rhythm and tone. The ' burden of the grasshopper' (a fine instance, this, of Mr Eliot's genius in borrowing), though a burden, potently evoked, of annihilation, has nevertheless its share of the religious emotion that pervades the poem. The ' garden where all love ends' is associated with the garden in which God walked ' in the cool of the day.' A religious sense of awe, an apprehension of the supernatural, seems to inform the desert where the bones are scattered.

As for the ' three white leopards,' they are not symbols needing interpretation ; they act directly, reinforcing the effect of ritual that we have noted in the verse and suggesting the mode of experience, the kind of spiritual exercise, to which *Ash-Wednesday* is devoted. They belong with the ' jewelled unicorns' that have bothered some critics in the fourth poem :

> Redeem
> The unread vision in the higher dream
> While jewelled unicorns draw by the gilded hearse.

Perhaps in this last passage Mr Eliot has been too helpful and ' the higher dream' is too like explicit elucidation. But it at any rate reminds us conveniently of certain things that he says in his

Dante. He remarks [1] of the ' pageantry ' of the *Paradise* :

> It belongs to the world of what I call the *high dream*, and the modern world seems capable only of the low dream.

And he says elsewhere : [2]

> Dante's is a *visual* imagination. It is a visual imagination in a different sense from that of a modern painter of still life : it is visual in the sense that he lived in an age in which men still saw visions. It was a psychological habit, the trick of which we have forgotten, but as good as any of our own. We have nothing but dreams, and we have forgotten that seeing visions—a practice now relegated to the aberrant and the uneducated—was once a more significant, interesting, and disciplined kind of dreaming.

When Mr Eliot says that we have forgotten the trick he means it. He no more supposes that Dante's mode of vision can be recaptured than that Dante's belief can. [3] But his frequentation of Dante has its place in that effort ' to construct something ' and that ' training of the soul ' [4] which he speaks of. And his leopards and unicorns seem to insist on the peculiar kind of ' disciplined dreaming ' that he strives to attain in ' the dreamcrossed twilight ' of *Ash-Wednesday*. They go with the formal quality of the verse, in

---

[1] *Dante*, p. 48.   [2] *Ibid.*, p. 23.
[3] See *A Note on Poetry and Belief* (*The Enemy*), Jan. 1927, p. 10.
[4] See above, p. 114.

which we have already noted a suggestion of ritual, and with the liturgical element, to define the plane at which this poetry works. The spiritual discipline is one with the poetical.

The third poem of the sequence offers an admirable example of the way in which Mr Eliot blends the reminiscent (literary or conventional) in imagery with the immediately evocative. The ' stairs ' of this poem (they have a ' banister ') have their effect for a reader who recognizes no reminiscence. They concentrate the suggestion of directed effort that distinguishes this poetry from the earlier, and they define the nature of the effort. The poem epitomizes, as it were, a spiritual history, and records a sense of an advance and a hardly-dared hope of attainment (qualified by the humility that becomes explicit at the end). But the stairs also recall the stairs of the *Purgatorio*—a reminiscence that is picked up again in the next poem, in a further quotation from that Provençal passage of Canto XXVI which Mr Eliot has used so much :

> Ara vos prec, per aquella valor
>   que vos guida al som de l'escalina,
>   sovegna vos a temps de ma dolor.[1]

This, in a new spirit, is the art that he practised in *The Waste Land*.

[1] ' Now I pray you, by that goodness which guideth you to the summit of the stairway, be mindful in due time of my pain.'—*Poi s'ascose nel foco che gli affina.*

The opening of the fourth poem recalls a
passage of the third, that giving the view through
the ' slotted window ' :

> . . . beyond the hawthorn blossom and a pasture
>   scene
> The broadbacked figure drest in blue and green
> Enchanted the maytime with an antique flute.
> Blown hair is sweet, brown hair over the mouth
>   blown,
> Lilac and brown hair . . .

This backward glimpse of youth ' where trees
flower and springs flow ' seems to be dismissed
here as ' distraction.' But the sense of refresh-
ment·that distinguishes the fourth poem seems to
owe something to the same source. The ' violet,'
the ' larkspur ' and the ' varied green ' have an
effect like that of ' lilac,' and she ' who walked '
may well have had brown hair. But this imagery,
which is directly evocative, also lends itself to
symbolic associations—

> Going in white and blue, in Mary's colour

and

> In blue of larkspur, blue of Mary's colour

—and she who ' made strong the fountains and
made fresh the springs ' takes on a specifically
religious significance. Is the poet remembering
an actual religious experience, or is he using the
memory of the time when the springs were fresh
as a symbol? The case is subtler. The un-

specified 'who' and the indeterminate syntax, together with the element of 'higher dream' that we have already discussed, and the

> White light folded, sheathed about her, folded,

intimate that the process here is analogous to that represented by Dante's Beatrice.[1] The 'yews' again are directly evocative : they have current values ; beneath them

> ghostly shapes
> May meet at noontide ; Fear and trembling Hope,
> Silence and Foresight ; Death the Skeleton
> And Time the Shadow

—though these yews, owing to the context, suggest a particular religious tradition.

A process analogous to Dante's ; but the modern poet can make no pretence to Dante's certitude—to his firm possession of his vision. The ambiguity that constructs a precarious base for rejoicing in the fourth poem brings doubt and fear of inner treachery in the fifth. The breath-

---

[1] See Santayana's *Poetry and Religion*, pp. 128-9 :

'Neither the conscious spell of the senses nor the affinities of taste and character can then be powerful, but the sense of loneliness and the vague need of loving may easily conspire with the innocence of the eyes to fix upon a single image and to make it the imaginary goal of all those instincts which as yet do not know themselves.

'When with time these instincts become explicit and select their respective objects, if the inmost heart still remains unsatisfied, as it must in all profound or imaginative natures, the name and memory of that vague early love may well subsist as a symbol for the perfect good yet unattained. . . . Having recognized that she was to his childish fancy what the ideals of religion were to his mature imagination, Dante intentionally fuses the two, as every poet intentionally fuses the general and the particular, the universal and the personal.'

less, circling, desperately pursuing movement of
the opening, with its repetitions and its play upon
' word,' ' Word,' ' world ' and ' whirled,' suggests
both the agonized effort to seize the unseizable,
and the elusive equivocations of the thing grasped.
The doubts and self-questionings are developed,
and the poem ends with a despairing recognition
of the equivocal that recalls, in a significant way,
the second poem :

> In the last desert between the last blue rocks
> The desert in the garden the garden in the desert
> Of drouth, spitting from the mouth the withered
>   apple-seed.
>
>   O my people.

In the earlier poem the desert that the bones
inherit—the ' garden where all love ends '—is
associated with the garden in which God walked
' in the cool of the day.' The ambiguity is the
condition of a poise between widely divergent
impulses and emotions that produces a strange
serenity. But here, in the fifth poem, we have
instead an equivocation of experience that produces agonizing doubt : which is garden and
which is desert ?

In the last poem of the sequence the doubt
becomes an adjuvant of spiritual discipline,
ministering to humility. But an essential ambiguity remains, an ambiguity inescapable

> In this brief transit where the dreams cross.

To symbolize, to conceive for himself, the spiritual order that he aspires towards, the poet inevitably has recourse to his most vital mundane experience. But the memories of this present themselves also as temptation, as incitement to subtle treacheries :

> . . . though I do not wish to wish these things
> From the wide window towards the granite shore
> The white sails still fly seaward, seaward flying
> Unbroken wings
>
> And the lost heart stiffens and rejoices
> In the lost lilac and the lost sea voices
> And the weak spirit quickens to rebel
> For the bent golden-rod and the lost sea smell. . . .

—The ' lost heart ' is itself ambiguous : the heart is ' lost ' because it succumbs to temptation and ' rebels ' ; but ' lost ' also records a pang of regret, a rebellious questioning of the renunciation : the heart is ' lost ' because it has lost the lilac and the sea voices. With ' merely vans to beat the air ' the poet looks enviously at the unbroken wings that fly seaward, and prays :

> Suffer us not to mock ourselves with falsehood.

In the *Ariel* poem that appeared after *Ash-Wednesday* it is Marina, who was lost and found again, who becomes the symbol for the new realization striven after. But this is to simplify too much. *Marina* belongs, like *Ash-Wednesday*, to ' the time of tension between dying and birth,'

I

and exhibits an even more subtle ambiguity than anything in the sequence. The liturgical note is absent, and one may indicate the change in rhythm by saying that it has about it nothing of ritual; yet the poem expresses something approaching nearer to assurance than anything in *Ash-Wednesday*. Images like the things that the poet 'did not wish to wish' now 'return,' bringing with them a sense of ineffable peace.

The coming of 'this grace' by which the various forms of death

> Are become unsubstantial, reduced by a wind,
> A breath of pine, and the woodsong fog

is associated with the approach of a ship to 'granite islands.' The 'white sails' and the 'granite shore' of *Ash-Wednesday* have taken another value here. The ship—'I made this'—represents the effort 'to construct something upon which to rejoice.' Marina, the daughter lost and recovered, evokes the peculiar sense of victory over death that attends upon 'this grace':

> This form, this face, this life
> Living to live in a world of time beyond me; let me
> Resign my life for this life, my speech for that unspoken,
> The awakened, lips parted, the hope, the new ships.

Just what is the nature of the new life we cannot say. It is an elusive apprehension, conveyed poignantly, but in essential ambiguities. The poem is the resultant of diverse suggestions and orientations. The imagery belongs to the ' higher dream ' :

> What is this face, less clear and clearer
> The pulse in the arm, less strong and stronger—
> Given or lent ? more distant than stars and nearer
>   than the eye . . .

The indeterminate syntax intimates the kind of relation that exists between the various elements of the poem : one would not, to put it crudely, think of trying to relate Marina, her father, the ship and the islands in a story. And the elusiveness of the relations suggests at the same time the felt transcendence of the vision and its precariousness.

The poetry of the last phase may lack the charged richness and the range of *Gerontion* and *The Waste Land*. But it is, perhaps, still more remarkable by reason of the strange and difficult regions of experience that it explores. Its association with Mr Eliot's explicit Anglo-Catholicism has encouraged, in the guise of criticism, an extraordinarily crude and superficial approach. Critics speak of ' Pre-Raphaelite imagery ' and a ' Pre-Raphaelite flavour ' and deplore (or applaud) the return to the fold. But this poetry is more disconcertingly modern than *The Waste Land* : the preoccupation with traditional Christianity, the use of the Prayer Book, and the devotion to spiritual discipline should not hinder the reader from seeing that the modes of feeling, apprehension and expression are such as we can find nowhere earlier. If it is likely to be significant for young poets, that is not because of the intellectual fashions that attribute so much importance to T. E. Hulme, but because contemporary poets are likely to find that the kind of consciousness represented by *Ash-Wednesday* and *Marina* has a close bearing upon certain problems of their own. It is not for nothing that in the field of critical thought—in the consideration of those general problems that literary criticism nowadays cannot ignore—Mr Eliot remains a directing influence.[1]

[1] See Review of *Science and Poetry* (I. A. Richards) in *The Dial*, March 1927. *The Enemy*, January 1927: *Note on Poetry and Belief*. *Dante*, T. S. Eliot. Note to Chap. II.

IV

Ezra Pound

MR POUND has been closely associated with Mr Eliot. Indeed, Mr Eliot acknowledges a debt to him :

> A man who devises new rhythms is a man who extends and refines our sensibility ; and that is not merely a matter of ' technique.' I have, in recent years, cursed Mr Pound often enough ; for I am never sure that I can call my verse my own ; just when I am most pleased with myself, I find that I have caught up some echo from a verse of Pound's.[1]

And more generally :

> He has enabled a few other persons, including myself, to improve their verse sense ; so that he has improved poetry through other men as well as by himself. I cannot think of any one writing verse, of our generation and the next, whose verse (if any good) has not been improved by the study of Pound's.[2]

—*The Waste Land*, we note, is inscribed to Ezra Pound, *il miglior fabbro*.

Mr Eliot's witness carries authority. It is nevertheless plain that when the history of the present phase of English poetry comes to be written, Mr Eliot will be adjudged to have made

[1] *The Dial*, January 1928 : article entitled *Isolated Superiority*.
[2] *Ibid*.

the decisive impact and to have opened the way :
whatever he and others may owe to Mr Pound,
the influence of Mr Pound that can be observed
from outside is secondary to Mr Eliot's. The
sponsoring by Mr Eliot of the volume of *Selected
Poems* is symbolic ; it does not misrepresent their
relations, in spite of the consciousness of a debt
to Mr Pound that has, not altogether happily,
inspired Mr Eliot's *Introduction*. Not altogether
happily, because this consciousness, together with
a generous concern to obtain for Mr Pound the
recognition due to him, seems accountable for a
certain uncritical deflection in Mr Eliot. No one
interested in poetry is quick to dissent from
Mr Eliot's judgment ; but the *Introduction* does
not represent his criticism at its best. The manner
itself sometimes makes us uneasy : it would before
have seemed impossible that Mr Eliot could ever
remind us, even remotely, of Mr G. K. Chesterton.
And there are places that pull us up short :

> It may give surprise that I attach so much im-
> portance to *Hugh Selwyn Mauberley*. This seems to
> me a great poem. . . . I know very well that the
> apparent roughness and *naïveté* of the verse and
> rhyming of *Mauberley* are inevitably the result of
> many years of hard work : if you cannot appreciate
> the dexterity of *Altaforte* you cannot appreciate the
> simplicity of *Mauberley*.[1]

It does not at all surprise me (in such a matter

[1] *Introduction* to *Selected Poems*, p. xxiii.

it is best to speak in the first person) that Mr Eliot
should find *Hugh Selwyn Mauberley* a great poem ;
but the last assertion does surprise me : it con-
flicts with my experience, and with the experience
of those with whom I discuss modern poetry.
Any one capable of profiting by Mr Eliot's
Introduction is, I should say, likely to find *Mauberley*
immediately convincing : the difficulty is to be
interested in the earlier work. One can see, of
course, that this was in a sense a necessary part of
Mr Pound's development, but I do not find it
(and I have been much corroborated here) a
necessary, or even helpful, approach to *Mauberley*.

Once, however, *Mauberley* has been accepted,
the earlier work offers some interest (again I
report my own experience). It shows what looks
like a representative start from the 'nineties : ' his
versification,' says Mr Eliot,[1] ' is a *logical* development of the verse of his English predecessors ' ;
and his substance is ' poetical.' Morris, Swinburne, Yeats make themselves felt, *Cynara*—

But for all that, I am homesick after mine own kind—
and the 'nineties generally. It is a Victorian
' romanticism,' a response (explicit in the poem [2]
just quoted) to the Victorian situation of the artist :

> And I am homesick
> After mine own kind that know, and feel
> And have some breath for beauty and the arts.

[1] *Introduction,* p. xi.   [2] *Selected Poems,* p. 20 (*In Durance*).

But the poet is not content with dreaming
                                how
  'Beyond, beyond, beyond, there lies . . .';

another influence, not yet mentioned, manifests itself strongly in his verse—that of Browning. Browning has much to do with the way in which the Provençal themes of *Personae* are handled : the poetic world is to be a 'real' world. But Mr Pound's Provence is none the less a form of romantic evasion : his Browning consorts quite happily with Mr Yeats.

It is, however, the versification that Mr Eliot stresses in his *Introduction*. Elsewhere (in the article in *The Dial* already quoted from) he says of Mr Pound :

> What is curious is his complete and isolated superiority as a master of verse form. No one living has practised the art of verse with such austerity and devotion ; and no one living has practised it with more success.

Mr Eliot's judgment in such a matter is authoritative. But in the same article (which reads much more like single-minded criticism than the *Introduction*) he also says :

> I confess that I am seldom interested in what he is saying, but only in the way he says it.

He may add : ' That does not mean that he is saying nothing ; for ways of saying nothing are not interesting ' ; but the interest has nevertheless been drastically limited. It is, perhaps, an interest that can be very significant only to a poet whom chance brought into early association with Mr Pound. At any rate, apart from some such happy chance, it seems improbable that a way of saying that can be so sharply distinguished from the thing said could do much towards re-orientating English poetry.

The distinction, as a matter of fact, seems to imply a criticism of the quality of Mr Pound's own interest in what he says. His various addictions—Provençal, Italian, Chinese—speak the amateur: one cannot doubt his seriousness or his enthusiasm, but something else, surely, was needed to impel significant innovations in poetry—and something more than a devotion to the art of verse. Even when, as in *Lustra* and after, he finds his themes in the contemporary world and writes consciously modern poems—

Here they stand without quaint devices,
Here they stand with nothing archaic about them

—his modern interests, one feels, are for him mainly opportunities, taken or made, for verse practice: his partiality for the epigram has its significance (this is not to condemn his epigrams by comparing them with the *Ode to a Nightingale*).[1]

---

[1] 'The reader who does not like Pound's epigrams should make very sure that he is not comparing them with the *Ode to a Nightingale* before he condemns them.'—*Introduction*, p. xix.

However, there are some memorable pieces, and
we have to recognize a growing subtlety in his
verse. His dropping of archaisms and poeticisms,
and his use of modern speech-idiom, are particularly interesting. But however remarkable the
achievement in verse may be, it is not such that
one could have foreseen *Mauberley* in it. Not to
insist on this is to be unfair to Mr Pound : it
might be urged against Mr Eliot that his generous
concern for justice has led him to minify the pre-
eminence of *Mauberley* when insistence on that
pre-eminence is needed to secure for Mr Pound
the attention he merits.

In *Mauberley* we feel a pressure of experience,
an impulsion from deep within. The verse is
extraordinarily subtle, and its subtlety is the
subtlety of the sensibility that it expresses. No
one would think here of distinguishing the way
of saying from the thing said. It is significant
that the pressure seems to derive (we are reminded
of Mr Yeats) from a recognition of bankruptcy, of
a devoted life summed up in futility. A study of
the earlier work, then, does at least help the commentary on *Mauberley* : it helps to bring out the
significance of the poem for the inquiry in hand.

Mauberley is in the first place (the description
suggests itself readily) the summing-up of an
individual life. It has also a representative value,
reflecting as it does the miscellaneousness of

modern culture, the absence of direction, of an
alphabet of forms or of any one predominant
idiom ; the uncongeniality of the modern world
to the artist ; and his dubious status there. It
offers, more particularly, a representative experience of the phase of English poetry in which it
became plain that the Romantic tradition was
exhausted. One might, at the risk of impertinence, call it quintessential autobiography, taking
care, however, to add that it has the impersonality
of great poetry : its technical perfection means a
complete detachment and control.

To enforce this account some kind of running
commentary is needed. But the more one
appreciates *Mauberley* the less happily does one
embark upon exposition : it seems impertinent to
explain what so incomparably explains itself, and
all elucidation looks crude. Yet *Mauberley* has
almost wholly escaped recognition, and one may
perhaps be too much afraid of dealing in the
obvious. At any rate, courage seems here the
better part of discretion.

The opening of the first poem of *Mauberley*
(which is more than a sequence) reminds us in
movement of certain things of Mr Eliot's :

> For three years, out of key with his time,
> He strove to resuscitate the dead art
> Of poetry ; to maintain ‘ the sublime ’
> In the old sense.   Wrong from the start—

> No, hardly, but seeing he had been born
> In a half-savage country, out of date ;
> Bent resolutely on wringing lilies from the acorn ;
> Capaneus ; trout for factitious bait

—the rhythm of this is curiously like that of the opening of *A Song for Simeon* :

> Lord, the Roman hyacinths are blooming in bowls and
> The winter sun creeps by the snow hills ;
> The stubborn season has made stand.
> My life is light, waiting for the death wind,
> Like a feather on the back of my hand.
> Dust in sunlight and memory in corners
> Wait for the wind that chills towards the dead land.

This may be an instance of the indebtedness to Mr Pound that Mr Eliot acknowledges (it is not often that we find an excuse for the conjecture). Less dubiously it illustrates a certain community of experience : it is not surprising that two poets, in the age that has been described, should have learnt to express so subtly by rhythmic means the break-down of rhythm.

But in essentials Mr Pound's poetry is very different from Mr Eliot's. There are in it none of Mr Eliot's complex intensities of concern about soul and body : the moral, religious and anthropological preoccupations are absent. Mr Pound's main concern has always been art : he is, in the most serious sense of the word, an aesthete. It is this that makes the peculiar nature of Mr Eliot's plea for the earlier work necessary. But here, in *Mauberley*, there is the pressure of personal experience. The title of the first poem, with its ironical allusion to Ronsard—*E. P. Ode Pour L'Election de Son Sepulchre*—is explicitly personal : it indicates what is to follow. The poet is looking back on a life devoted to the cultivation of aesthetic fastidiousness, technical perfection, exquisite eclecticism. He is no longer trying to resuscitate the dead art of poetry, or observing the elegance of Circe's hair; he is taking stock, and what has it all amounted to ? What is the outcome ? He touches various notes, plays on various themes, and recalls various representative memories in the different constituent poems. The poems together form one poem, a representative experience of life—tragedy, comedy, pathos and irony. And throughout there is a subtlety of tone, a complexity of attitude, such as we associate with seventeenth-century wit.

In this first poem he conveys, with masterly compression, the nature of the interests and attitudes that have occupied his life. The ironically sublime comparison of himself to Capaneus, the hero who defied the gods and paid the penalty, has its comment in the contemptuous contrasting image : ' trout for factitious bait '— the stake a mere gaudy fly, and a faked one at that. The Homeric quotation suggests his romantic

addiction to the classics and the past : his ear
has been unstopped to too many Sirens.

His true Penelope was Flaubert

—In all his romantic excursions he has remained
constant to one faith, the aesthetic : his main
concern has been art, art as represented by
Flaubert, saint and martyr of the artistic conscience.

He fished by obstinate isles

suggests his inveterate eclecticism, his interest in
various periods and cultures, Provençal, Italian,
Chinese, classical and so on. He has always

> Observed the elegance of Circe's hair
> Rather than the mottoes on sundials.

He has devoted his life to aesthetic discrimination
and technical perfection while life slipped by.
Life now has, it seems, slipped by, and what has
come of it all ? The last stanza answers with an
oblique reference to Villon, the unfastidious
blackguard whose ' wasted ' life produced so rich
a harvest of poetry. His own industrious career,
on the contrary, our poet sees as yielding

No adjunct to the Muses' diadem.

Nevertheless, this disillusioned summing-up is
itself great poetry, ' criticism of life ' in the best
sense of the phrase, as Mr Eliot says. For

Mr Pound has not been unaffected by the march of all events. However uncongenial one may find his eclectic aestheticism, his devotion to the elegance of Circe's hair, it has been accompanied by intense seriousness : Mr Pound is not an American for nothing. What we have in *Mauberley* is a representative sensibility, that of a poet who found his starting point in the 'nineties, lived through the heavy late-Victorian years of Edward VII, saw his friends disappear in the war, and now knows that the past holds more for him than the future.

His technical skill is now a matter of bringing to precise definition a mature and complex sensibility. The rhythms, in their apparent looseness and carelessness, are marvels of subtlety : ' out of key with his time ' is being said everywhere by strict rhythmic means. What looks like the free run of contemporary speech achieves effects of a greater precision than can be found very often in *The Oxford Book*. And the verse has extraordinary variety. The subtlety of movement is associated with subtlety of mood and attitude. 'Wit' is present. Critical activity accompanies feeling and remembering. Mr Pound can be, as the seventeenth-century poets were, serious and light at the same time, sardonic and poignant, flippant and intense.

Devices that might easily degenerate into tricks

(' stunts ') remain under perfect control.   Take,
for example, the use of inverted commas :

> Unaffected by ' the march of events '
>
> The ' age demanded ' chiefly a mould in plaster,
> Made with no loss of time,
> A prose kinema, not, not assuredly, alabaster
> Or the ' sculpture ' of rhyme.
>
> The tea-rose tea-gown, etc.
> Supplants the mousseline of Cos,
> The pianola ' replaces '
> Sappho's barbitos.
>
> Incapable of the least utterance or composition,
> Emendation, conservation of the ' better tradition ',
> Refinement of medium, elimination of superfluities,
> August attraction or concentration.

To be able to use such a device as freely as
Mr Pound does without prejudice to subtlety of
tone and emphasis is to pass a severe test.   His
poise, though so varied, and for all his audacities,
is sure ; how sure, nothing can show better than
the pun in the last stanza of the third poem :

> O bright Apollo,
> Τίν' ἀνδρα, τίν' ἥρωα, τίνα θεὸν,
> What god, man, or hero
> Shall I place a tin wreath upon !

In what poet, after the seventeenth century, can
we find anything like this contributing to a
completely serious effect (the poem is not only
tragically serious but solemn).

The second and third poems introduce the

modern world of mass-production and levelling-down, a world that has destroyed the traditions and is hostile, not only to the artist, but to all distinction of spirit. The fourth and fifth poems bring in the war. They are a more remarkable achievement than they may perhaps at first appear to be.

> Died some, pro patria,
> non ' dulce ' non ' et decor ' . . .
> walked eye-deep in hell
> believing in old men's lies, then unbelieving
> came home, home to a lie,
> home to many deceits,
> home to old lies and new infamy ;
> usury age-old and age-thick
> and liars in public places.

—That is a dangerous note, and only the completest integrity and the surest touch could safely venture it. But we have no uneasiness. The poet has realized the war with the completely adult (and very uncommon) awareness that makes it impossible to nurse indignation and horror. *Mauberley* came out in 1920. The presence of the war in it, we feel, is not confined to these two small poems : they are not mere detachable items. They represent a criterion of seriousness and purity of intention that is implicit in the whole. To say this is to indicate the gulf between any of the earlier work, archaizing or modernizing, and *Mauberley*.

In *Yeux Glauques*, the next piece, we hark back
to the age of peace and prosperity that prepared
the war; the phase of English culture out of
which the poets of the 'nineties started. Pre-
Raphaelite art with, for setting, Gladstone,
Ruskin and Victorian morality on the one hand,
and Swinburne, Rossetti and Victorian immorality
on the other. Next, in ' *Siena mi fe ; disfecemi
Maremma*,' we have the 'nineties themselves with
their blend of religion, religiosity, aestheticism
and dissipation :

> For two hours he talked of Gallifet ;
> Of Dowson ; of the Rhymers' Club ;
> Told me how Johnson (Lionel) died
> By falling from a high stool in a pub . . .
>
> But showed no trace of alcohol
> At the autopsy, privately performed—
> Tissue preserved—the pure mind
> Arose toward Newman as the whisky warmed.

The irony of this might be called flippant : if so,
it is a flippancy that subserves a tragic effect.
Nothing could illustrate more forcibly Mr Pound's
sureness of touch, his subtle mastery of tone and
accent. The poem is one of the most daring
things in the sequence—though ' daring ' might
suggest a possible qualm about it : it is justified
by complete success. Rhythmically it is consummate ; but that must be said of *Mauberley* as
a whole, in all its rich variety. Mr Pound's
rhythmic suppleness continually surprises.

In *Mr Nixon* he gets new effects out of colloquial speech.   It is sardonic comedy; the
theme, Success in modern letters.   Mr Pound's
earlier satiric verse is always technically adroit
and often amusing; but no one would have
thought the author capable of a satiric note that
should be in keeping with tragic seriousness.
Mr Nixon is.   That is enough to say by way of
emphasizing the distinction of the achievement.

Numbers X and XI might have appeared in
Lustra, though they have their place here in the
context of the whole.   But XII exhibits again
technical mastery functioning at the highest level.
It is another marvel of tone and poise.   The movement is extraordinarily varied, and the tempo and
modulation are exquisitely controlled.   The theme
is another aspect of modern letters: elegant
patronage, modish dilettantism.—

.   .   .   .

> Conduct, on the other hand, the soul
> ' Which the highest cultures have nourished '
> To Fleet St. where
> Dr Johnson flourished ;
>
> Beside this thoroughfare
> The sale of half-hose has
> Long since superseded the cultivation of
> Pierian roses.

—For the author, what is the actuality, what does
it all come to, but journalism, the all-absorbing,

which hardly any talent nowadays escapes ? The trade of writing could once support a Johnson. It is now commercial in senses and at levels inconceivable in Johnson's time.

The *Envoi* that follows sets off the subtlety of Mr Pound's rhythmic inventions by a masterly handling of canorous lyric measures that can be chanted at sight. This lovely little poem, which will hardly escape the anthologist when he discovers it, I have found useful in convincing the classically-trained that Mr Pound's metrical irregularities are not the result of incompetence.

The section called *Mauberley*, which occupies the remaining five pages of the fifteen, brings the personal focus of the whole to sharp definition.

> ' Qu'est ce qu'ils savent de l'amour, et qu'est ce qu'ils peuvent comprendre ?
>
> ' S'ils ne comprennent pas la poésie, s'ils ne sentent pas la musique, qu'est ce qu'ils peuvent comprendre de cette passion en comparaison avec laquelle la rose est grossière et le parfum des violettes un tonnerre ? '

—So, with implicit irony, runs the epigraph to the second poem of the section. The habit of disinterested aesthetic contemplation, of observing the elegance of Circe's hair rather than the mottoes on sundials, takes on a tragic significance. The poem is poignantly personal, and yet, in its technical perfection, its ironical economy, im-

personal and detached. Consider, for instance,
the consummate reserve of this :

> Unable in the supervening blankness
> To sift TO AGATHON from the chaff
> Until he found his sieve . . .
> Ultimately, his seismograph :

—With what subtle force the shift of image in the
last line registers the realization that the ' orchid '
was something more, the impact more than
aesthetic ! And with what inevitability the
' seismograph ' and the scientific terminology and
manner of what follows convey the bitter irony of
realization in retrospect ! Mr Pound's regeneration of poetic idiom is more than a matter of using
modern colloquial speech :

> He had passed, inconscient, full gaze,
> The wide-banded irides
> And Botticellian sprays implied
> In their diastasis ;
>
> Which anaesthesis, noted a year late,
> And weighed, revealed his great affect,
> (Orchid), mandate
> Of Eros, a retrospect.

It is a contemporary sensibility that expresses the
futile bitterness of this recognition in this air of
scientific detachment, of disinterested scrutiny.
The last stanza evokes directly the sense of frus-
trate emptiness in a reference to Ovid (Metamor-
phoses VII), the image of the dogs turned to
stone in the act of seizing the quarry.

The next poem, ' *The Age Demanded,*' has much
the same theme, more generalized : the penalty
for absorption in aesthetic contemplation, for too
much concern with fineness of living ; the unfit-
ness for survival of the artist in the modern world,
the world of Lady Valentine, and the world
which follows

> The discouraging doctrine of chances

preached by Mr Nixon. The poem is not difficult, unless rhythmically (the state of education in
poetry being what it is), and comment will serve
no purpose. Along with the preceding one it
represents the summit of Mr Pound's superbly
supple and varied art.

But *Hugh Selwyn Mauberley*, it must be repeated,
is a whole. The whole is great poetry, at once
traditional and original. Mr Pound's standing as
a poet rests upon it, and rests securely. The
earlier poems have a minor kind of interest, and
(to revert to the first person of modesty) I do not
think that it is a service to the poet or the reader
to insist upon them. They have the kind of
bearing upon *Mauberley* that has been indicated :
they help the commentator. And in them, clearly,
Mr Pound developed his technique. It is interesting to follow this development, but not in the
least necessary. If the earlier poems are read at
all with profit it is likely to be because of *Mauber-*

ley, which will convince, if at all, by itself, and is in itself capable of being a decisive influence. That it has already been such the last chapter will offer evidence.

Since *Mauberley* the *Cantos* have, at various times, appeared, the latest collection being *A Draft of XXX Cantos*.[1] Again I find myself embarrassed by the necessity of disagreeing with Mr Eliot. One gathers from the *Introduction*[2] to *Selected Poems* that he regards the *Cantos* as being an advance upon *Mauberley*:

> The closest approximation—I mean the most nearly continuous identification—of form and feeling in Pound's poetry, I find in his *Cantos*, of which I can say but little, as I am not permitted to print them in this book. (At least, they are the only ' poem of some length ' by any of my contemporaries that I can read with enjoyment and admiration; at most, they are more than I could deal with anyway in this essay; in any case, they are a mine for juvenile poets to quarry; and in any case, my disagreement with their ' philosophy ' is another affair.)

It is to be regretted that Mr Eliot has not found time to deal with them somewhere. In the article, *Isolated Superiority*, already referred to, he is indeed more explicit about the ' philosophy ':

> As for the meaning of the *Cantos*, that never worries me, and I do not believe that I care. I know that Pound has a scheme and a kind of philo-

---

[1] Hours Press, Paris, 1930.   [2] See p. xxii.

sophy behind it; it is quite enough for me that he thinks he knows what he is doing; I am glad that the philosophy is there, but I am not interested in it.

This hardly leaves the commentary at a more satisfactory point. Mr Eliot's pronouncement on the value of Mr Pound's work to juvenile poets, its value as ' an inexhaustible reference book of verse form,' [1] it is not for me to question. But he does seem to have limited very drastically the kind of importance that can be attributed to the *Cantos*— more drastically than comports with the effect of his allusions to them in the *Introduction*. It is possible to understand that a poet already strongly impelled, and already definitely orientated, might profit by studying verse form as such. But the influence of verse form so abstracted can hardly be of the order of significance represented by *Mauberley*, which might very well launch a young poet. In any case, it is a kind of influence that I do not know how to take account of.

The possible interest in verse form so distinguishable from interesting communication seems extremely limited. ' I confess that I am seldom interested in what he is saying, but only in the way he says it. That does not mean that he is saying nothing; for ways of saying nothing are

---

[1] ' I cannot think of any one writing verse, of our generation and the next, whose verse (if any good) has not been improved by a study of Pound's. His poetry is an inexhaustible reference book of verse form. There is, in fact, no one else to study.'—*Isolated Superiority*.

not interesting.' And surely, one may add, the interestingness of ways of saying depends a great deal upon the quality of what is said. ' Swinburne's form,' goes on Mr Eliot, ' is uninteresting, because he is literally saying next to nothing. . . .' —I am afraid that often in reading the *Cantos* I feel as if what is being said were not much better than nothing.

I am the more emboldened to report my experience and publish my conclusion since, while Mr Eliot has not been more explicit, other critics who have written on the *Cantos* seem to have adopted his assurance as to their value without being able to say why. The critic whose essay was printed in *The Criterion* for April 1931, does indeed tell us, among a great deal that does not appear to mean very much, that Mr Pound ' is closely related in method and spirit to the kind of ideation found in Dante's Divine Comedy.' [' As are : T. S. Eliot in *The Waste Land* ; E. E. Cummings in *Him* ; and perhaps one other American, at least in intention.'—Footnote.] It does not seem likely that Mr Eliot would endorse this account.

The reviewer in *The Hound and Horn* (Winter, 1931) appears more concerned to be intelligible ; but again it is hard to believe that the various ' contrapuntal ' and ' harmonic ' effects that he analyses are what chiefly interests Mr Eliot in the

Cantos. It is not that one finds any difficulty in seeing what Mr Pound is at : it is fairly obvious. The reviewer just mentioned puts it in this way :

> Mr Pound's documentation is a device, a technic. History and literature are for him a mine of images, and his purpose is to fix certain of these images in a lasting, orderly design, without reference to a philosophy or to any system of teleological principles. Now whether the historical fact, the Image, be the blowing of apricot-blossoms from east to west, or a narcotic charge preferred against Frank Robert Iriquois of Oklahoma City, or the departure of Anchises from Troy, it is a detail of supreme importance to the frieze, a note of supreme importance to the *mélos*, which is the poem as a whole. The poet, as I have observed, uses images precisely as another poet would use metaphors or, even more simply, chromatic words. These images have no ' hidden ' meaning. Malatesta, Frank Robert Iriquois, the apricot blossoms, are no more ' puzzling ' than Shakespeare's ' encarnadine ' in the verse about the multitudinous seas. It is true that if you have enough Latin to be able to associate ' encarnadine ' with ' flesh,' ' carnation,' and the other rich, warm *carn* words, you will derive more enjoyment from the verse than will X, who knows only that ' encarnadine ' is a euphemism for ' redden '; but you will ' understand ' the verse not a whit better than your less informed friend. Therefore, the criticism that *XXX Cantos* is incomprehensible is a false criticism ; and I have gone into it at some length simply because it seems to be the objection that is being most strongly urged against the poem. The *Cantos* will baffle persons who are willing to be

baffled ; but this is so in the case of any considerable poem.

The *Cantos* may be described as an epic of timelessness. That is to say, the poem represents Mr Pound's endeavour to manage an arrest of time. Roughly the method is that of identification or fusion of image. . . .'

—Without any willingness to be baffled one may reply that while one ' understands ' readily enough, the ' understanding ' one has of a very large part of the *Cantos* amounts to a good deal less than knowing that ' encarnadine ' means ' redden.' When Mr Eliot in *The Waste Land* has recourse to allusion, the intrinsic power of his verse is commonly such as to affect even a reader who does not recognize what is being alluded to. But even when one is fully informed about Mr Pound's allusions one's recognition has no significant effect : the value remains private to the author. The methods of association and contrast employed in *The Waste Land* subserve an urgency pressing from below : only an austere and deep seriousness could have controlled them into significance. But the *Cantos* appear to be little more than a game—a game serious with the seriousness of pedantry. We may recognize what Mr Pound's counters stand for, but they remain counters ; and his patterns are not very interesting, even as schematic design, since, in the nature of the game, which hasn't much in the way of rules ('without reference to a philosophy or to any system of teleological principles'), they lack definition and salience.

The radical criticism is made, oddly enough, by this same reviewer in the end of his review, as a kind of unimportant afterthought :

> . . . But he has failed to convey these associations to the reader. For the moment he is indulging in pure pedantry—and not very accurate pedantry at that. Again he has ceased to assert ; he has substituted something unconvincingly dead for something convincingly alive. And I would suggest that this tendency is fundamental. Mr Pound's attitude *is* the pedantic, unreal attitude. Throughout the book he has substituted book-living for actual living.

The judgment seems to me just and damning. The *Cantos* are the kind of ' poem of some length ' to which, looking back, we can see that the early work (apart from *Mauberley*) points. They are Mr Pound's *The Ring and the Book*. In so far as they have a representative significance it is as reflecting the contemporary plight that has already been discussed—the lack of form, grammar, principle and direction. To compel significant art out of that plight needed the seriousness, the spiritual and moral intensity, and the resolute intelligence that are behind *The Waste Land*. Mr Pound's kind of seriousness is not enough. The very nature of the recognition that (deepened by the war [1]) turned him into a major poet in *Mauberley* seems to constitute a presumption against success in such an undertaking as the *Cantos*.

All this insistence must appear ungracious. But it seems to me the only way of being just to Mr Pound—to put the stress in a still more important place, the most hopeful way of getting *Mauberley* recognized for the great poem it is.

[1] See especially, ' *There died a myriad* ' (V).

V

Gerard Manley Hopkins

GERARD MANLEY HOPKINS died in
1889. He was one of the most remarkable
technical inventors who ever wrote, and he was a
major poet. Had he received the attention that
was his due the history of English poetry from
the 'nineties onward would have been very different. But that is a fanciful proposition : it would
be extravagant to suppose that he would have
received such attention even had his poems been
generally accessible. Even now that they have
been so for a dozen years, we see that it is possible
for respected critics, writing about them with the
consciousness of authority, to exhibit conspicu-
ously in public a complete and complacent obtuse-
ness, and yet arouse no remark : that is the
measure of Hopkins's originality. It is, however,
difficult not to believe that if the poems had been
current they would have fertilized some young
talent and we should not now be contemplating
the futility of the Georgian attempt to regenerate
English poetry. But they were not published as
a body until 1918. To explain how thirty years
of potential influence were thus lost is a delicate

undertaking ; it is best left, perhaps, to the poet's biographer, Father Lahey [1] :

> The staunch love and the highest literary apprecia-
> tion of him who was admittedly the best custodian
> of the poems, prevented Dr Bridges from flooding
> an unappreciative and uncomprehending literary
> public with the rays of so original a source of pure
> poetry, so that he bided his time and with careful
> discrimination slowly educated his future readers
> with selections given to anthologies.   After almost
> thirty years of patient waiting he published the
> slender volume of poems to which were added his
> own notes, the creative criticism of a delicate poetic
> sensibility.

These notes continue the education of the reader by laying down firmly the limits within which the poet is to be approved, and do the poet the further service of discounting adverse criticism by insisting on it.   In the following [2] Dr Bridges raises radical issues :

> Apart, I say, from such faults of taste ['occasional
> affectation in metaphor,' 'perverted Marianism,'
> etc.], which few as they numerically are yet affect my
> liking and more repel my sympathy than do all the
> rude shocks of his purely artistic wantonness—
> apart from these there are definite faults of style
> which a reader must have courage to face, and must
> in some measure condone before he can discover
> the great beauties.   For these blemishes in the
> poet's style are of such quality and magnitude as to

---

[1] *Gerard Manley Hopkins*, G. F. Lahey, S.J., p. 16.
[2] *Poems of Gerard Manley Hopkins*.   Second Edition, p. 96 (the references that follow are all to the Second Edition).

deny him even a hearing from those who love a continuous literary decorum and are grown to be intolerant of its absence.   And it is well to be clear that there is no pretence to reverse the condemnation of those faults, for which the poet has duly suffered.   The extravagances are and will remain what they were.   Nor can credit be gained from pointing them out : yet, to put readers at their ease, I will here define them : they may be called Oddity and Obscurity ; and since the first may provoke laughter when a writer is serious (and this poet is always serious), while the latter must prevent him from being understood (and this poet has always something to say), it may be assumed that they were not a part of his intention.

A great deal is too readily assumed here : it is possible to put readers of Hopkins too much at their ease.   The ' obscurity ' is, in a sense to be explained later, intended.   The ' oddity,' as Dr Bridges goes on to show, Hopkins was aware of ; but he felt that too big a price might be paid for the approval of ' those who love a continuous literary decorum.'   What Dr Bridges calls ' blemishes ' are essential to Hopkins's aim and achievement ; it is difficult to understand how the attitude implicit in this description of them can go with an interest in his work.   Dr Bridges quotes from the poet's letters :

' No doubt my poetry errs on the side of oddness. I hope in time to have a more balanced and Miltonic style.   But as air, melody, is what strikes me most of all in music and design in painting, so design, pattern, or what I am in the habit of calling *inscape*, is what I above all aim at in poetry. Now it is the virtue of design, pattern, or inscape to be distinctive and it is the vice of distinctiveness to become queer. This vice I cannot have escaped.' And again two months later: 'Moreover the oddness may make them repulsive at first and yet Lang might have liked them on a second reading. Indeed, when, on somebody returning me the *Eurydice*, I opened and read some lines, as one commonly reads whether prose or verse, with the eyes, so to say, only, it struck me aghast with a kind of raw nakedness and unmitigated violence I was unprepared for: but take breath and read it with the ears, as I always wish to be read, and my verse becomes all right.'

But that 'love of a continuous literary decorum' stood in the way. Such a decorum, like Good Form, has its uses; but both become cramping absurdities when erected into ultimate ends. That Hopkins's experiments should not have been obviously reasonable and obviously justified by a considerable measure of success shows how badly they were needed. He aimed to get out of his words as much as possible unhampered by the rules of grammar, syntax and common usage. But to the late Dr Bridges, as to so many people, these rules were ends in themselves. He complains that in Hopkins one often has to determine the grammar by the meaning, 'whereas the grammar should expose and enforce the meaning, not have to be determined by the meaning.'—

' Should ' : one is reminded of *les jeunes* who discuss whether Mr Eliot's methods in *The Waste
Land* are ' legitimate ' or not, when the only question worth discussing is, Do they work ?

But it is only fair to Dr Bridges to admit that it
is not the indecorum alone that he objects to :

> Here, then, is another source of the poet's
> obscurity ; that in aiming at condensation he
> neglects the need that there is for care in the plac-
> ing of words that are grammatically ambiguous.
> English swarms with words that have one identical
> form for substantive, adjective and verb ; and such
> a word should never be so placed as to allow of any
> doubt as to what part of speech it is used for ;
> because such ambiguity or momentary uncertainty
> destroys the force of the sentence. Now our
> author not only neglects this essential propriety but
> he would seem even to welcome and seek artistic
> effect in the consequent confusion ; and he will
> sometimes so arrange such words that a reader
> looking for a verb may find that he has two or three
> ambiguous monosyllables from which to select, and
> must be in doubt as to which promises best to give
> any meaning that he can welcome ; and then, after
> his choice is made, he may be left with some home-
> less monosyllable still on his hands. Nor is our
> author apparently sensitive to the irrelevant sugges-
> tions that our numerous homophones cause ; and
> he will provoke further ambiguities or obscurities by
> straining the meaning of these unfortunate words.

This criticism assumes that poetry ought to be
immediately comprehensible. But Hopkins felt
no obligation to subscribe to that particular notion

of Good Form. ' Writers,' says Dr Bridges, ' who
carelessly rely on their elliptical speech-forms to
govern the elaborate sentences of their literary
composition little know what conscious effort of
interpretation they often impose on their readers.
But it was not carelessness in Gerard Hopkins. . . .'
—Nor can Hopkins have been unaware that he
imposed a conscious effort of interpretation upon
his readers.   It is true that he felt that his critics
exaggerated the difficulty of his verse : ' The
sonnet (I say it snorting) aims at being intelligible.' [1]   Or rather, he felt that with an effort
that might be fairly demanded he *could* be understood, and that it was not at intrinsic difficulties
alone that they were boggling. For he must
deliberately have contemplated leaving the reader
in more than momentary uncertainty : he had
positive uses for ambiguity, and he presumed to
expect from the reader prolonged and repeated
intellectual effort. A great many people who
fancy themselves interested in poetry resent such
an expectation : very few are prepared to make
any effort at all.   I have heard it announced in a
cultivated drawing-room that the choruses from
Gilbert Murray's Euripides are some of the
finest poetry in the language. But Hopkins is
very unlike his contemporary, Swinburne. Hopkins is really difficult, and the difficulty is essential.

[1] *Poems*, p. 118. Cf. ' O, once explained, how clear it all is ! ' p. 115.

If we could deceive ourselves into believing that we were reading easily his purpose would be defeated ; for every word in one of his important poems is doing a great deal more work than almost any word in a poem of Robert Bridges. If (as Mr I. A. Richards pointed out [1] in what appears to have been the first intelligent critique of Hopkins) we were allowed to slip easily over the page, the extremely complex response called for would not have a chance to develop. The final, adequate reading will not be a matter of arduous struggle (though a sense of tension and resistance is usually an essential part of the effect), but it will have been made possible by previous intellectual effort, the condition of various subtle and complex organizations.

Hopkins, as Dr Bridges points out, did not take to obscurity and oddity because of any incapacity for the conventional forms. He practised verse-writing from an early age, and wrote prize poems while at school. These are remarkably accomplished, but, in the relation that they exhibit to Keats, Shelley, Byron and Tennyson, normal products of the period. Having, while at Oxford, become a Catholic, he entered the Order of Jesus, and gave up poetry for some time :

What (verses) I had written I burnt before I became a Jesuit (*i.e.* 1868) and resolved to write no

[1] *The Dial*, September 1926.

more, as not belonging to my profession, unless it were by the wish of my superiors ; so for seven years I wrote nothing but two or three little presentation pieces which occasion called for. But when in the winter of '75 the *Deutschland* was wrecked in the mouth of the Thames and five Franciscan nuns, exiles from Germany by the Falck Laws, aboard of her were drowned I was affected by the account and happening to say so to my rector he said that he wished some one would write a poem on the subject. On this hint I set to work and, though my hand was out at first, produced one. I had long had haunting my ear the echo of a new rhythm which now I realised on paper. . . . I do not say the idea is altogether new . . . but no one has professedly used it and made it the principle throughout, that I know of. . . . However, I had to mark the stresses . . . and a great many more oddnesses could but dismay an editor's eye, so that when I offered it to our magazine, *The Month* . . . they dared not print it.[1]

Hopkins went on with his experiments, sending his poems for criticism to his friends Robert Bridges and Canon Dixon. His friends, it appears, stood unwearyingly to the defence of a continuous literary decorum. But Hopkins knew what he was trying to do, and without encouragement, in this complete isolation, kept on his path. He was a man of rare character as well as intelligence. He writes [2] in reply to one can guess what kind of suggestion : ' The effect of studying

[1] *Poems of Gerard Manley Hopkins*, p. 102.   [2] *Ibid.*, p. 118.

masterpieces is to make me admire and do otherwise.   So it must be on every original artist to
some degree, on me to a marked degree.   Perhaps
then more reading would only *refine my singularity*,
which is not what you want.'—Self-sureness of
that kind (it was justified) is genius.

Hopkins's originality was radical and uncom-
promising : there was, as he owns, some excuse
for the dismay of his first readers.   He could not
himself, as the *Author's Preface* shows, be reconciled to his originality without subterfuge.   His
prosodic account in terms of Logaoedic Rhythm,
Counterpoint Rhythm, Sprung Rhythm, Rocking
Feet and Outriders will help no one to read his
verse—unless by giving the sense of being helped :
it merely shows how subtle and hard to escape is
the power of habits and preconceptions.   The
prescription he gives when warm from reading his
verse—' take breath and read it with the ears, as
I always wish to be read, and my verse becomes all
right '—is a great deal more to the point, and if we
add ' and with the brains and the body ' it suffices.

This is a measure of the genuineness of his
originality.[1]   For the peculiarities of his technique
appeal for sanction to the spirit of the language :

---

[1] ' The poem which is absolutely original is absolutely bad ; it is,
in the bad sense, " subjective " with no relation to the world to which
it appeals.

' Originality, in other words, is by no means a simple idea in the
criticism of poetry.   True originality is merely development.'—
T. S. Eliot, *Selected Poems : Ezra Pound, Introduction*, p. x.

his innovations accentuate and develop bents it exhibits in living use and, above all, in the writings of the greatest master who ever used it. Hopkins might have said about each one of his technical idiosyncrasies what he says about the rhythm of *The Wreck of the Deutschland*: the idea was not altogether new, but no one had professedly used it and made it a principle throughout as he had. Paradoxical as it may sound to say so, his strength was that he brought poetry much closer to living speech. How badly some such regeneration was needed may be judged from the inability of critics avowedly interested in him, as Bridges and Dixon were, to appreciate his significance: the habits and conventions he defeated were so strong. They are strong still: Mr Charles Williams, the editor of the second edition of the *Poems*, concludes in his *Critical Introduction* that the 'poet to whom we should most relate Gerard Hopkins' is Milton. Now if one were seeking to define the significance of Hopkins by contraries, Milton is the poet to whom one would have recourse: the relation is an antithesis. But, alas! Mr Williams leaves no room to suppose that he means that.

The way in which Hopkins uses the English language (that is the primary order of consideration; 'consciousness of the universe'[1] is an

---

[1] 'The simultaneous consciousness of a controlled universe, and yet of division, conflict, and crises within that universe, is hardly so

unprofitable abstraction apart from it) contrasts
him with Milton and associates him with Shakespeare.   There is no essential characteristic of his
technique of which it might not be said that it is
a matter of ' using professedly ' and ' making a
principle ' of something that may be found in
Shakespeare :

> . . . the world-without-end hour [1]

> > . . . bloody, bawdy villain !
> Remorseless, treacherous, lecherous kindless vil-
> lain ! [2]

> . . . cabin'd, cribb'd, confined [3]

> > what thou wouldst highly,
> That wouldst thou holily. [4]

> If it were done when 'tis done, then 'twere well
> It were done quickly : if the assassination
> Could trammel up the consequence, and catch
> With his surcease success ; that but this blow
> Might be the be-all and the end-all here,
> But here, upon this bank and shoal of time,
> We'd jump the life to come. [5]

—This last passage takes us beyond technical
devices, found in embryo in Shakespeare.   Indeed,
it would be a mistake to insist too much on these
(they could be exemplified indefinitely) ; it might
distract attention from the more essential likeness
illustrated by the passage as a whole.   Hopkins's

poignantly expressed in any other English poets than those two.'—
Poems of Gerard Manley Hopkins, Introduction, p. xiv.
[1] *Sonnet* 57.   [2] *Hamlet*, II. ii.   [3] *Macbeth*, III. iv.
[4] *Macbeth*, I. v.   [5] *Macbeth*, I. vii.

imagery, and his way of using the body and movement of the language, are like Shakespeare's.

> O the mind, mind has mountains ; cliffs of fall
> Frightful, sheer, no-man-fathomed. Hold them
>   cheap
> May who ne'er hung there. Nor does long our small
> Durance deal with that steep or deep.[1]

—That is Shakespearian, but quite un-Miltonic.
And this ('what's not meet' being made to suggest at the same time 'not what's meet') handles
grammar and syntax in the spirit of Hopkins :

>   In a rebellion,
> When what's not meet, but what must be, was law,
> Then were they chosen : in a better hour,
> Let what is meet be said it must be meet,
> And throw their power in the dust.[2]

If we look for a parallel to a characteristic Shakespearian rendering of the very movement of
consciousness—

> My thought, whose murder yet is but fantastical,
> Shakes so my single state of man, that function
> Is smother'd in surmise, and nothing is,
> But what is not [3]

—we shall find it easily in Hopkins :

>   Only what word
> Wisest my heart breeds dark heaven's baffling ban
> Bars or hell's spell thwarts.   This to hoard unheard,
> Heard unheeded, leaves me a lonely began.[4]

It is not that he derives from Shakespeare

---

[1] *Poems of Gerard Manley Hopkins*, p. 62.   [2] *Coriolanus*, III. i.
[3] *Macbeth*, I. iii.   [4] *Poems*, p. 65.

(Shakespeare, we have often been told, is a dangerous model). We cannot doubt that he knew his Shakespeare well, but if he profited he was able to do so because of his own direct interest in the English language as a living thing. The bent of his genius was so strong that we are forced to believe that his experimenting would have taken much the same lines even if there had been no Shakespeare. The similarities arise out of a similar exploitation of the resources and potentialities of the language. Hopkins belongs with Shakespeare, Donne, Eliot and the later Yeats as opposed to Spenser, Milton and Tennyson.[1] He departs very widely from current idiom (as Shakespeare did), but nevertheless current idiom is, as it were, the presiding spirit in his dialect, and he uses his medium not as a literary but as a spoken one. That is the significance of his repeated demand to be tested by reading aloud : ' read it with the ears, as I always wish to be read, and my verse becomes all right.' [2] It is not merely the rhythm that he has in mind :

> I laughed outright and often, but very sardonically, to think you and the Canon could not construe my last sonnet ; that he had to write to you for a crib. It is plain I must go no further on this road : if you and he cannot understand me who will ? Yet, declaimed, the strange constructions would be dramatic and effective.[3]

[1] Cf. p. 81.   [2] *Poems of Gerard Manley Hopkins*, p. 97.   [3] *Ibid.*, p. 114.

It is not only the constructions that gain, and the term ' dramatic ' has a further sense here than perhaps Hopkins intended. His words and phrases are actions as well as sounds, ideas and images, and must, as I have said, be read with the body as well as with the eye : that is the force of his concern to be read aloud. He indicates now and then in notes the kind of thing he is doing. ' Here comes a violent but effective hyperbaton or suspension, in which the action of the mind mimics that of the labourer—surveys his lot, low but free from care ; then by a sudden strong act throws it over the shoulder or tosses it away as a light matter.' [1]—Effects of this order may be found on any page of his work. Even more significant is a note on a word in *The Leaden Echo and the Golden Echo*. It is the more interesting in that Mr Sturge Moore paid this poem some attention in a recent number of *The Criterion*.[2] The poem opens :

How to kéep—is there ány any, is there none such,
    nowhere known some, bow or brooch or braid
    or brace, láce, latch or catch or key to keep
Back beauty, keep it, beauty, beauty, beauty, . . .
    from vanishing away ?

[1] *Poems of Gerard Manley Hopkins*, p. 115. For an analogous effect, cf.:
               ' On a huge hill,
Cragged, and steep, Truth stands, and hee that will
Reach her, about must, and about must goe ;
And what the hills suddennes resists, winne so : '
                       Donne, *Satyre* III.

[2] *Criterion*, July 1930.

Hopkins notes [1] : ' *Back* is not pretty, but it gives that feeling of physical constraint which I want.' This suggests fairly the spirit of his dealings with the English language.   How alien to English poetry that spirit had become is illustrated by Mr Sturge Moore, a critic and verse-writer formed in the last century, who, writing on *Style and Beauty in Literature*, offers to improve Hopkins in this way :

> How to keep beauty ? is there any way ?
> Is there nowhere any means to have it stay ?
> Will no bow or brooch or braid,
> Brace or lace
> Latch or catch
> Or key to lock the door lend aid
> Before beauty vanishes away ?

There is no need to quote further.   No reader of *The Criterion*, apparently, protested.   Mr Sturge Moore remarks at the end that he has retained most of Hopkins's felicities, while discarding ' his most ludicrous redundancies.'   He has discarded also ' back ' and everything it represents ; words as he uses them have no body.   He has discarded, not merely a certain amount of music, but with the emotional crescendo and diminuendo, the plangent rise and fall, all the action and substance of the verse.

Not that *The Leaden Echo and the Golden Echo* is one of the poems in which the poet's greatness

[1] *Poems of Gerard Manley Hopkins*, p. 113.

manifests itself.   Remarkable as it is, if it were
fully representative of Hopkins he would not
demand much space in this study.   In this kind
of work he is elaborating and mastering his technical devices for more important purposes.   It
is not as mere musical effects (if such were possible in poetry)—melody, harmony, counterpoint
—that these devices are important; they are
capable of use for expressing complexities of feeling, the movement of consciousness, difficult and
urgent states of mind.   Take for instance the
kind of word-play, the pattern and progression of
verbal echo, alliteration, rime and assonance
represented in the opening verse :

> How to kéep—is there ány any, is there none such,
>   nowhere known some, bow or brooch or braid
>   or brace, láce, latch or catch or key to keep
> Back beauty . . .

—That need not be (indeed, is not) a mere musical
trick, any more than conventional end-rime need
be.   Such devices may be used, as good poets use
end-rime, to increase the expectancy involved in
rhythm and change its direction, to control movement, to give words new associations and bring
diverse ideas and emotions together, to intensify
the sense of inevitability—in short, to get new,
precise and complex responses out of words.

Of course, to be something convincingly more
than word-play, to escape the limiting description,

' music,' these devices must have adequate work
to do. The theme of *The Leaden Echo and the
Golden Echo* does not offer very much resistance,
and if this poem represented the height of Hopkins's achievement Mr Middleton Murry's judgment [1] would not be immediately absurd : ' If one
were to seek in English the lyrical poem to which
Hopkins's definition [' The roll, the rise, the carol,
the creation '] could be most fittingly applied, one
would find Shelley's *Skylark*. A technical progression onwards from the *Skylark* is accordingly
the main line of Hopkins's poetical evolution.'
But if one looks at *The Wreck of the Deutschland*,
which, says Bridges, ' stands logically as well as
chronologically in the front of his book, like a
great dragon to forbid all entrance,' it becomes
plain that Hopkins has no relation to Shelley or
to any nineteenth-century poet. This poem was
his first ambitious experiment, and it is the more
interesting in that his technical resources are
deployed in it at great length : the association of
inner, spiritual, emotional stress with physical
reverberations, nervous and muscular tensions
that characterizes his best verse is here explicitly
elaborated in an account of the storm which is at

---

[1] *Aspects of Literature*, p. 55. It is only fair to say that Mr Murry's
essay was written in the circumstances of weekly journalism. In those
circumstances to have written seriously and at length on Hopkins
must go on the credit side of a critic's account. *Aspects of Literature*
contains some of the best criticism of modern poetry that has
appeared.

the same time an account of an inner drama.   The
wreck he describes is both occasion and symbol.
He realizes it so vividly that he is in it ; and it is
at the same time in him :

> I did say yes
> O at lightning and lashed rod ;
> Thou heardst me truer than tongue confess
> Thy terror, O Christ, O God ;
> Thou knowest the walls, altar and hour and night:
> The swoon of a heart that the sweep and the hurl
> of thee trod
> Hard down with a horror of height :
> And the midriff astrain with leaning of, laced with
> fire of stress.

He takes the actual wreck as the type of the worldly
disaster that brings conviction, supernatural assurance, to the soul :

> Stroke and a stress that stars and storms deliver,
> That guilt is hushed by, hearts are flushed by, and
> melt

—and identifies such experience mystically with
Christ's Passion.   In an audacious image he
identifies the sudden overwhelming conviction,
the insight, the illumination to the effect of a sloe
bursting in the mouth :

> The dense and driven Passion, and frightful
> sweat ;
> Thence the discharge of it, there its swelling to be,
> Though felt before, though in high flood yet—
> What none would have known of it, only the heart,
> being hard at bay,

Is out with it! Oh,
We lash with the best or worst
Word last! How a lush-kept plush-capped
    sloe
Will, mouthed to flesh-burst,
Gush!—flush the man, the being with it, sour or
    sweet,
Brim, in a flash, full!—Hither then, last or first,
To hero of Calvary, Christ's feet—
Never ask if meaning it, wanting it, warned of it—
    men go.

The conceit is Metaphysical, but the technique is pure Hopkins. It would be difficult to produce a more elaborate pattern of alliteration, echo, assonance and internal rime, but we do not feel of any element (except, perhaps, ' lush-kept plush-capped ') that it is there for the sake of pattern. Even of ' lush-kept plush-capped ' it might be said that by a kind of verbal suggestion (two different expressions sounding so like) it contributes to the sense of mystical identification that the passage is concerned to evoke—identification of ' the stress felt ' with the Passion ; helps also the metaphorical identification of the experience with the bursting of the sloe. Of the pattern generally it may be said that it issues out of and expresses emotional intensities in the same kind of way as ' cabin'd, cribb'd, confined ' and

bloody, bawdy villain !
Remorseless, treacherous, lecherous, kindless villain !

M

and

> . . . trammel up the consequence, and catch
> With his surcease success.

Particularly it may be pointed out how the words stressed by the pattern justify their salience.

> Is out with it !   Oh,
> We lash with the best or worst
> Word last !

—'lash' (the highly-stressed 'out' carries on from the previous line) both suggests the inevitability (a lashing out on the stimulus of pain) of the response at this supreme testing moment ('last'), and gives the response a physical urgency. The moment is ripe ('lush') : and 'lush' applied to 'sloe' also suggests the paradoxical poignancy ('sour or sweet' ?) of the revelation.   In 'flesh-burst' we have both the physical disaster 'that storms deliver' and Calvary.   The progression —'gush,' 'flush,' 'flash,' 'full'—is as much a matter of sense as sound : 'gush' describes the overwhelming onset of the experience, 'flush' the immediate bewildering immersion ; 'flash' —it becomes illumination ; 'full' suggests 'cup.'

Such an analysis is clumsy and inadequate : it is merely a means of indicating the kind of function that the more obvious technical devices serve. What Hopkins does here in this sustained and elaborated way he does in concentration in *The Windhover* and *Spelt from Sibyl's Leaves*.

Imagery that reminds us still more readily of the Metaphysical conceit (the characteristic Hopkins pattern is less insistent here) occurs in the fourth stanza :

> I am soft sift
> In an hourglass—at the wall
> Fast, but mined with a motion, a drift,
> And it crowds and it combs to the fall ;
> I steady as a water in a well, to a poise, to a pane,
> But roped with, always, all the way down from
> the tall
> Fells or flanks of the voel, a vein
> Of the gospel proffer, a pressure, a principle, Christ's
> gift.

—The superb metaphor in the first part of the stanza offers no difficulty. It conveys perfectly the inner sinking and dissolution, and then (with a subtle shift from sand to water) the steadying and recovery. The imagery in the last three lines is more complex, but, when (from the notes) we know that ' voel ' is Welsh for ' bare hill,' not too difficult. The note adds : ' the meaning, obscured by *roped*, is that the well is fed by trickles of water within the flanks of the mountains.' This brief elucidation is a useful foil to the strength of Hopkins's imagery. The ' obscured ' should imply no adverse criticism : the metaphorical ' roped ' may make the original passage less immediately intelligible than Bridges' summary, but it also makes the mountain-rill something far more suggestive of power than a trickle, something capable of exerting pressure; it also suggests, illogically but not incompatibly (it is often the business of metaphor to reconcile opposed impulses, bents or emotions), that the 'pressure,' the 'principle,' can draw upwards. Nothing approaching this imagery in subtlety and strength can be found in any other poet of the nineteenth century.

Hopkins's technique justifies itself equally in the description of the storm in the second part of the poem—justifies itself obviously. Indeed, Bridges' 'dragon' exaggerates the general difficulty: a great deal of the poem is as inviting to the anthologist as the first stanza, which he printed in *The Spirit of Man*. The first stanza of the second part, for instance, is even less refractory to 'the grand style of our poetry':

> 'Some find me a sword; some
>   The flange and the rail; flame,
> Fang, or flood' goes Death on drum,
>   And storms bugle his fame.
>   But wé dream we are rooted in earth—Dust!
>   Flesh falls within sight of us, we, though our
>   flower the same,
>   Wave with the meadow, forgèt that there must
> The sour scythe cringe, and the blear share come.

(The last line has six stresses.)

But remarkable as *The Wreck of the Deutschland* is it does not put his technical skill to the utmost stretch. This skill is most unmistakably that of a great poet when it is at the service of a more immediately personal urgency, when it expresses not religious exaltation, but inner debate. *The Windhover* is a poem of this kind. Since not only Mr Richards, in the essay [1] already mentioned, but Mr Empson also, in *Seven Types of Ambiguity*,[2] have dealt admirably with this poem, there is no need to analyse it here. Mr Empson's book is one that nobody interested in English poetry can afford not to have read. It is an implicit commentary on Bridges' complaint that ' ambiguity or momentary uncertainty destroys the force of the sentence ' [3] and imposes on the reader a ' conscious effort of interpretation.' [4] The kind of ambiguity that Mr Empson finds to be the essence of *The Windhover* is suggested here : ' Thus in the first three lines of the sestet we seem to have a clear case of the Freudian use of opposites, where two things thought of as incompatible, but desired intensely by different systems of judgments, are spoken of simultaneously by words applying to both ; both desires are thus given a transient and exhausting satisfaction, and the two systems of judgment are forced into open conflict before the reader.' It is in place at this point

[1] See p. 165.
[2] *Seven Types of Ambiguity*, W. Empson, p. 284 ff.
[3] *Poems of Gerard Manley Hopkins*, p. 98.
[4] *Ibid.*, p. 97.

to observe that Hopkins's genius was as much a matter of rare character, intelligence and sincerity as of technical skill : indeed, in his great poetry the distinction disappears ; the technical triumph is a triumph of spirit.

The inner friction expressed in the equivocal burden of *The Windhover* comes out more explicitly in *Spelt from Sibyl's Leaves*, which, if it represents a less difficult undertaking, is more indubitably a complete success. It is one of the finest things that he ever did, and since it exhibits and magnificently justifies most of the peculiarities of his technique, I will (though Mr Richards has analysed it) venture a brief commentary :

> Earnest, earthless, equal, attuneable, | vaulty, volu-
> minous, . . stupendous
> Evening strains to be tíme's vást, | womb-of-all,
> home-of-all, hearse-of-all night.
> Her fond yellow hornlight wound to the west, | her
> wild hollow hoarlight hung to the height
> Waste ; her earliest stars, earl-stars, | stárs principal,
> overbend us,
> Fíre-féaturing heaven. For earth | her being has
> unbound, her dapple is at an end, as-
> tray or aswarm, all throughther, in throngs ; | self
> ín self steepèd and páshed—qúite
> Disremembering, dísmémbering | áll now. Heart,
> you round me right
> With : Óur évening is over us ; óur night | whélms,
> whélms, ánd will end us.
> Only the beak-leaved boughs dragonish | damask
> the tool-smooth bleak light ; black,

Ever so black on it.   Our tale, O óur oracle ! | Lét
    life, wáned, ah lét life wind
Off hér once skéined stained véined varíety | upon,
    áll on twó spools ;   párt, pen, páck
Now her áll in twó flocks, twó folds—black, white; |
    right, wrong ;   reckon but, reck but, mind
But thése two ;   wáre of a wórld where bút these |
    twó tell, each off the óther ;   of a rack
Where, selfwrung, selfstrung, sheathe- and shelter-
    less, | thóughts agaínst thoughts ín groans
    grínd.

The poem opens with evening deepening into
night.   We are not merely told that evening
' strains,' we feel evening straining, to become
night, enveloping everything, in the movement,
the progression of alliteration, assonance and
rime.   This progression is associated with, and
hardly distinguishable from, the development of
meaning in the sequence of adjectives : evening
is first sweetly solemn, serene, etherealizing and
harmonizing, then becomes less tranquillizing and
more awful, and finally ends in the blackness of
night.

Her fond yellow hornlight wound to the west, her
    wild hollow hoarlight hung to the height
Waste . . .

—The ' yellow hornlight ' is, of course, the
setting moon ; ' fond '—tender, soft, sympathetic,
clinging as if reluctant to go, the slow gentle
sinking being felt in the movement and modula-

tion of the verse. The 'hoarlight' is the cold, hard starlight, 'wild' and 'hollow'—remote, inhuman, a kind of emptiness in the hollow vault —in contrast to the 'fond yellow' moonlight. The verse-movement itself, with the inevitable rest upon 'height,' seems to hang. The 'dapple' of earth, the rich coloured variety that Hopkins loved so much (cf. *Pied Beauty* [1]—' Glory be to God for dappled things ') has gone, merged (' throughther '—each through other) into neutrality. That he is not concerned with ' pure description ' the introduction of ' self ' intimates, together with the unexpected strength of ' steepèd and páshed ' and ' dismembering.'

He suddenly realizes the whole thing as a parable, not meditatively worked out, but immediate : he sees the outward symbol and the significance as one, in a kind of metaphor. It is Blake's *Sun-flower* rather than Matthew Arnold's *Yes : in the sea of life enisled.*

> Heart, you round me right
> With : Óur évening is over us ; oúr night whélms

—the heavy stress that his rhythm enables him to put upon ' our ' brings home the poignant realization. His heart ' rounds ' him, i.e. whispers (as in the ballads), and ' rounds upon him ' with, the thought that he has sacrificed the ' dapple '

[1] *Poems of Gerard Manley Hopkins,* p. 30.

of existence for the stark dichotomy of right and wrong.

> Only the beak-leaved boughs dragonish | damask
>   the tool-smooth bleak light; black,
> Ever so black on it.

—The trees are no longer the beautiful, refreshing things of daylight; they have turned fantastically strange, hard and cruel, ' beak-leaved ' suggesting the cold, hard light, steely like the gleam of polished tools, against which they appear as a kind of damascene-work ('damask') on a blade. Then follows the anguished surrender to the realization :

> . . . Oúr tale, O oúr oracle ! | Lét life, wáned, ah
>   lét life wind
> Off hér one skéined stained véined varíety | upon,
>   áll on twó spools ; párt, pen, páck
> Now her áll in twó flocks, twó folds—black, white; |
>   right, wrong . . .

—The run of alliterations, rimes and assonances suggests the irresistible poignancy of the realization. The poem ends with a terrible effect as of unsheathed nerves grinding upon one another. The grinding might at first be taken to be merely that of ' right ' against ' wrong,' the inner conflict of spirit and flesh, and the pain that which the believer knows he must face, the simple pain of renunciation. Yet we are aware of a more subtle anguish and a more desperate plight. And if we look closely we find that Hopkins is explicit about it :

> black, white ; right, wrong . . .

—The first draft had ' wrong, right,' but he deliberately, and significantly, reversed the order. If he were merely ' ware of a world where but these two tell ' his torment would be less cruel. But his consciousness is more complex; his absolutes waver and change places, and he is left in terrible doubt.

In comparison with such a poem of Hopkins's as this, any other poetry of the nineteenth century is seen to be using only a very small part of the resources of the English language. His words seem to have substance, and to be made of a great variety of stuffs. Their potencies are correspondingly greater for subtle and delicate communication. The intellectual and spiritual anaemia of Victorian poetry is indistinguishable from its lack of body. Hopkins is a very different poet from Dante, but a remark that Mr Eliot throws out [1] in the discussion of Dante has a bearing here : ' that Hell, though a state, is a state which can only be thought of, and perhaps only experienced, by the projection of sensory images ; and that the resurrection of the body has perhaps a deeper meaning than we understand.' The critical implications of this (they can be generalized and

[1] *Dante*, p. 32.

discussed apart from any theological context)
deserve pondering. They relate to another remark
of Mr Eliot's that has been quoted already and
applies also to Hopkins : in his verse ' the intellect
is at the tip of the senses.' And along with the
qualities indicated by this phrase goes a remarkable control of tempo and modulation.

The poems of Hopkins that stand in best hope
of general acceptance (after *Margaret*) are the
group of intensely personal sonnets that he wrote
towards the end of his life. *The Windhover* and
Spelt from Sibyl's Leaves are in sonnet-form, but
the late sonnets are immediately recognizable
as such. Moreover they lack anything in the
nature of

The roll, the rise, the carol, the creation,

for the pressure of personal anguish was too
strong ; and consequently they do not present so
formidable an appearance as where the Hopkins
technique is more copiously elaborated. As
Bridges put it,[1] when Hopkins died ' he was
beginning to concentrate the force of all his
luxuriant experiments in rhythm and diction, and
castigate his art into a more reserved style.' The
austerity was rather, perhaps, the effect of that
cruel inner friction expressed in *The Windhover*
and *Spelt from Sibyl's Leaves*. In spite of the

[1] *Poems of Gerard Manley Hopkins*, p. 99.

terrible import of these poems there is still a
certain magnificent buoyancy in the handling of
the technical problems.   But when he wrote those
last sonnets Hopkins had no buoyancy left.   They
are the more interesting from the point of view of
this study in that they bring out more plainly the
relation of his medium to speech.   More obviously
here than in the more canorous poems the ruling
spirit is that of living idiom ;   we can hear the
speaking voice :

> I wake and feel the fell of dark, not day.
> What hours, O what black hoürs we have spent
> This night ! what sights you, heart, saw ; ways
>   you went !
> And more must, in yet longer light's delay.
>   With witness I speak this.   But where I say
> Hours I mean years, mean life.   And my lament
> Is cries countless, cries like dead letters sent
> To dearest him that lives alas ! away.

Yet this is characteristic Hopkins in its methods
of compression and its elimination of all in-
essential words.   There is the familiar use of
assonance :   ' feel ' becomes ' fell,' i.e. feeling
becomes an obsessing sense of the overwhelming
darkness (the adjectival homonym is felt in ' fell,'
which is therefore the smothering coat of a fell
beast) ;   and the sequence ' night,' ' sights,'
' light's ' suggest the obsessing horror of the
night.

There are a few difficulties ; notably, for in-

stance, in the sestet of the sonnet (47) that begins :
My own heart let me have more pity on. This is
admirably dealt with in *A Survey of Modernist
Poetry* [1] by Laura Riding and Robert Graves
(p. 90 ff.). But the difficulty will mainly be, not
to get the sense, but to realize the full effect intended, to get the ' oddities ' into focus. Some
of the effects are extremely subtle and original.
One of the most remarkable has already been
quoted :

> Only what word
> Wisest my heart breeds dark heaven's baffling ban
> Bars or hell's spell thwarts. This to hoard un-
>   heard,
> Heard unheeded, leaves me a lonely began.

This conveys the very process of frustration,
the very realizing of failure. No poet with a
respect for literary decorum could have accepted
that ' began ' even if it had come ;. but it is
magnificently justified. The passage, with all its
compression, achieved by characteristic means,
suggests the speaking voice using modern idiom :
' word wisest ' has nothing in common with
ordinary poetic inversion. And it would be hard
to illustrate better the difference between Hopkins's use of alliteration and assonance and
Swinburne's : in Hopkins they serve to call the
maximum attention to each word.

---

[1] This is a very uneven book. The authors, for instance, discuss
Hopkins and E. E. Cummings with equal gravity.

Another particularly remarkable effect is the
close of the sonnet called *Carrion Comfort* :

> That night, that year
> Of now done darkness I wretch lay wrestling with
>   (my God !) my God.

This, as the sonnet is read through, is completely
successful : it represents fairly the control, the
sureness of touch, and the perfection of essential
decorum that accompany Hopkins's audacities.

Yet training in the other decorum may cause a
great deal of boggling.   For example, the sonnet
The Candle Indoors (not one of the ' terrible ' ones)
begins :

> Some candle clear burns somewhere I come by,
> I muse at how its being puts blissful back
> With yellowy moisture mild night's blear-all black,
> Or to-fro tender trambeams truckle at the eye.

Of the last line the editor of the second edition of
the *Poems* remarks :

> It is perfectly possible to smile at the line, but
> hardly possible to laugh ; or only sympathetically,
> as at the wilder images of the metaphysicals, the
> extremer rhetoric of Marlowe, the more sedate
> elegances of Pope, the more prosaic moralities of
> the Victorians, or the more morbid pedestrianisms
> of Thomas Hardy.   Such things are the accidents
> of genius seriously engaged upon its own business,
> and not so apt as the observer to see how funny it
> looks.

And yet, once the meaning has been taken, there
should be nothing funny about the line.   The

image is so just, the expression of it, far from producing any accidental effect, so inevitable and adequate, that we hardly see the words as such; the image replaces them.   Hopkins is describing the lines of light (caused, I believe, by the eye-lashes) that, in the circumstances specified, con-verge upon the eye like so many sets of tram-rails. But ' tram ' unqualified would suggest something too solid, so he adds ' tender ' ; and ' truckle ' conveys perfectly the obsequious way in which they follow every motion of the eyes and of the eyelids.

Bridges, again, boggled at the second couplet of *Margaret*, and, in printing this poem (probably Hopkins's best-known) in *The Spirit of Man*, left it out.   I have heard him commended for the improvement.   The sonnet addressed to him perhaps he may be excused for venturing to correct.   It opens (as printed by him and Mr Williams) :

The fine delight that fathers thought ; the strong
Spur, live and lancing like the blowpipe flame,
Breathes once and, quenchèd faster than it came,
Leaves yet the mind a mother of immortal song.
Nine months she then, nay years, nine years she long
Within her wears, bears, cares and moulds the same:

—Bridges notes : ' In line 6 the word *moulds* was substituted by me for *combs* of original, when the sonnet was published by Miles ; and I leave it, having no doubt that G. M. H. would have made some such alteration.' Others will have considerable doubt. To use so weak a word as 'moulds' in this place is most unlike Hopkins. The objection to 'combs' seems to be based on nothing better than a narrow conception of metaphor—the same misconception that prompts editors to emend the ' To-morrow and to-morrow and to-morrow ' passage in *Macbeth* : '. . . having regard to the turn of thought and the necessary continuity of metaphors, I am convinced that Shakespeare's epithet was *dusky*.' [1] Good metaphor need not be a matter of consistently worked out analogy or point-for-point parallel; and the shift represented by 'combs' imposes itself as 'right' on the unprejudiced sensibility, and is very characteristic of Hopkins. Perhaps the term *prolepsis*, suitably invoked, would suffice to settle any qualms.

The strength and subtlety of his imagery are proof of his genius. But Victorian critics were not familiar with such qualities in the verse of their time. The acceptance of Hopkins would alone have been enough to reconstitute their poetic criteria. But he was not published in 1889. He is now felt to be a contemporary, and his influence is likely to be great. It will not necessarily manifest itself in imitation of the more

[1] *Macbeth: The Arden Shakespeare*, p. 141.

obvious of his technical peculiarities (these, plainly, may be dangerous toys); but no one can come from studying his work without an extended notion of the resources of English. And a technique so much concerned with inner division, friction, and psychological complexities in general has a special bearing on the problems of contemporary poetry.

He is likely to prove, for our time and the future, the only influential poet of the Victorian age, and he seems to me the greatest.

VI

Epilogue

THESE three poets whose work has been considered at length—Eliot, Pound and Hopkins—together represent a decisive re-ordering of the tradition of English poetry. If Mr Eliot stood alone it might be less obvious that his achievement constituted a new start. But when Mr Eliot is associated with two poets so unlike him and each other as Hopkins and Pound (but related to him in significance as suggested) the young practitioner, at any rate, cannot help being aware that his effort must be determined by bearings very different from the Victorian. The fact, too, that Mr Eliot is not alone makes his influence easier to escape from, and so more valuable.

This is not in the least to qualify the account suggested earlier of the decisiveness of Mr Eliot's achievement. Future English poetry (if English poetry is to continue) is likely to bear the same kind of relation to him as later Romantic poetry did to Wordsworth and Coleridge, but for whom Keats and Shelley, though quite unlike Wordsworth and Coleridge, would possibly not have been poets at all, or if they had been would certainly not have been the poets we know. It is owing to Mr Eliot that Pound and Hopkins can be discussed as having the significance here attributed to them, and can be associated with him in terms of a revised tradition.

That Mr Eliot could be so decisive shows, of course, that he was not a mere individual in isolation : he had a more important kind of originality. He was more aware of the general plight than his contemporaries, and more articulate : he made himself (answering to our account of the important poet) the consciousness of his age, and he did this the more effectively in that he was a critic as well as a poet. (A like alliance of creation and criticism is to be found in Wordsworth and Coleridge ; indeed we may expect to find them closely associated in any period in which tradition has failed the artist and needs to be radically revised.) Conclusive evidence of the debt to Mr Eliot is to be found in *The Calendar*, the review that has been mentioned in the *Prefatory Note*. That review enjoyed the services of a remarkably distinguished band of young critics, critics extremely intelligent and independent. Their review was very different in tone and spirit from *The Criterion* (sometimes bellicosely), but everywhere that they discuss modern poetry the debt is undisguised : it is assumed, implicitly and explicitly, that the general awareness of the important issues derives from Mr Eliot, and that the inevitable formulations are his.   There could be no more convincing testimony.   So to have crystallized the issues is an incalculable service, and Mr Eliot, as we have seen, has done more.

What, it will be asked, after this talk of a revised tradition and a new start, has come of it all—what follows ?   And looking round at the scene of young intellectuals dividing their admiration between Mr Eliot and Mr E. E. Cummings (though it must be admitted that one need hardly, any longer, add ' and the Sitwells '), being laboriously and eclectically parasitic upon the various phases of Mr Eliot's poetry, and getting beyond Mr Eliot, one feels some embarrassment.   Since Miss Nancy Cunard produced in *Parallax*[1] her simple imitation of *The Waste Land*, Mr Eliot has suffered a great deal of discipleship of varying degrees of *naïveté* and subtlety.   At the older universities his poetry has been reduced to a *procédé* with which not wholly unintelligent young men proceed confidently and with much cerebration to make poetry of their own.   Indeed this game has been played so assiduously and with, at a certain level, such plausibility, that it has become a nuisance and even something of a menace : it queers the pitch for serious work, and has, it may be suspected, beguiled a certain amount of

[1] Hogarth Press, 1925.

young talent into something worse than waste
of time.

No innovator is safe from such discipleship, and
Mr Eliot is to be commiserated upon it : it is
impossible where his influence is real. The significant kind of relation to him is illustrated by the
half-a-dozen remarkable poems that Mr William
Empson contributed to *Cambridge Poetry 1929*.
Mr Empson's poetry is quite unlike Mr Eliot's,
but without the creative stir and the re-orientation
produced by Mr Eliot it would not have been
written. One of his poems, *Arachne*, opens :

> Twixt devil and deep sea, man hacks his caves ;
> Birth, death ; one, many ; what is true, and seems ;
> Earth's vast hot iron, cold space's empty waves.

> King spider, walks the velvet roof of streams ;
> Must bird and fish, must god and beast avoid ;
> Dance, like nine angels, on pin-point extremes.

Mr Empson is not often as like Donne as this, but
he has clearly learnt a great deal from Donne.
And his debt to Donne is at the same time a debt
to Mr Eliot. It is not for nothing that Mr Eliot's
criticism has been directed mainly upon the
seventeenth century. One might say that the
effect of his criticism and his poetry together has
been to establish the seventeenth century in its
due place in the English tradition. In the seventeenth century (at any rate in the tradition deriving
from Donne) it was assumed that a poet should

be a man of distinguished intelligence, and he was encouraged by the conventions to bring into his poetry the varied interests of his life. Mr Empson's importance is that he is a very intelligent man with an intense interest, not only in emotions and words, but also in ideas and the sciences, and that he has acquired enough mastery of technique to write poetry in which all this is apparent. That such poetry should appear a few years after Mr Eliot's *Homage to John Dryden* (which deals mainly with the Metaphysicals) needs no long commentary.

At this point it is convenient to recall Warton's rhetorical question, quoted in the introductory chapter of this book, concerning Donne. Donne was a man of sense and a man of wit, but what traces had he left of Pure Poetry ? This attitude towards him has, in essentials, persisted to this day. Even in *The Oxford Book of English Verse* he has only as much space as Edward Robert Bulwer Lytton, Earl of Lytton, and less than a third as much as Herrick. I once pointed out this last fact to some one who had lectured on Donne, and it did not strike him as at all odd. My suggestion that Donne was indisputably a major poet and Herrick only a minor came to him as a new idea. In this he was a representative cultivated person of his generation : I can think of nothing that brings home more forcibly the strength and mischievousness of the tradition that is now seen to be dead. Those who see it to be dead see also, it is safe to say, that Donne is a major poet, and *vice versa*. Those to whom the propositions advanced in this book about the poetry of the nineteenth century seem arbitrary (and perhaps insolent) nonsense, will, if they are interested in Donne, apologize a great deal for him, judge him a very faulty craftsman whose verse is harsh and rugged, praise him for incidental poetical beauties achieved at great expense, and perhaps prefer his prose to his poetry. To those sympathetic to the point of view of this book Donne is one of the greatest masters of technique who ever lived.

But it will not do to let this reference to Donne imply a misleading account of Mr Empson. He is very original: not only his ideas but his attitude towards them and his treatment of them are modern. The wit for which his poetry is remarkable is modern, and highly characteristic. He writes, in *Legal Fiction*:

> Law makes long spokes of the short stakes of men.
> Your well fenced out real estate of mind
> No high flat of the nomad citizen
> Looks over, or train leaves behind.
>
> Your rights extend under and above your claim
> Without bound; you own land in Heaven and Hell;
> Your part is of earth's surface and mass the same,
> Of all cosmos' volume, and all stars as well.

Your rights reach down where all owners meet, in
    Hell's
Pointed exclusive conclave, at earth's centre . . .

He can be more subtle and complex in tone and
attitude than this : I should like to quote *To an
Old Lady*. But the little book of *Cambridge Poetry
1929* is cheap,[1] and all Mr Empson's poems are
worth attention. He is often difficult, and sometimes, I think, unjustifiably so ; but his verse
always has a rich and strongly characteristic life,
for he is as intensely interested in his technique
as in his ideas.

Indeed the criticism of him would be that in
his work the heat of creation is as yet too ex-
clusively a matter of interest in technique and
ideas ; and that, however intense this interest may
be, something more is needed before his intelligence and his technical skill can be fully employed,
and before one can predict for him confidently a
career as a poet. His published output is very
small. But even a very small achievement of that
kind deserves, in the present phase of English
poetry, the closest attention.

There is another young poet whose achieved
work leaves no room for doubt about his future.
Mr Ronald Bottrall's development has been remarkably rapid and sure—it is convincing—and
his published volume, *The Loosening and Other*

[1] Hogarth Press, 3s. 6d.

Poems,[1] establishes him as a very considerable poet indeed.   The poem from which the stanzas printed as epigraph to this book were chosen— *The Thyrsus Retipped*—is one of the earliest in his fully personal manner :

> Nightingales, Anangke, a sunset or the meanest
>   flower
> Were formerly the potentialities of poetry,
> But now what have they to do with one another
> With Dionysus or with me ?
>
> Drawn for a time towards inept vivisection
> I learned to air profundity in a comment
> As well by understudying Joyce as Valéry,
> Both sorting ill with my bent.

Obviously the study of *Hugh Selwyn Mauberley* was decisive for Mr Bottrall.   But his debt to Mr Pound serves to bring out his own strong originality : it takes unusual independence to learn in this way.   He is radically unlike Mr Pound, though Mr Pound's rhythms started him on the path to the solution of his own technical problems.   The difference comes out unmistakably even in this early poem.   The fourth stanza runs :

> Microscopic anatomy of ephemerides,
> Power-house stacks, girder-ribs, provide a crude
>   base ;
> But man is what he eats, and they are not bred
> Flesh of our flesh, being unrelated
> Experientially, fused in no emotive furnace.

[1] Minority Press (Agent : Heffer, Cambridge), 3s. 6d.

Mr Bottrall's use of a technical idiom and manner owes a great deal to Mr Pound, but in Mr Bottrall idiom and manner have a great deal more behind them.   He started, not as a poet of the 'nineties, but in the post-war world of power-house stacks and girder-ribs with its intellectual background— the world that presses so inescapably upon the intelligent and sensitive to-day.   The apparatus of this world associates itself with his most significant experience, he expresses himself naturally in ideas and imagery from the sciences ; in spite of his disclaimer, the technical element in his idiom is indeed ' related experientially,' ' fused ' in the ' emotive furnace.'

When, like Pound, he expresses his sense of the uncongeniality, the hostility of the modern world to the artist and the sensitive in general, we feel a stronger drive, both emotional and intellectual, in his verse than in Pound's :

> The gimlet eye has its own penalties
> Greater than its rewards ; the span and scope
> Of our thought-engined levitation, levered thrice
> Over by integrity's crowbar-thrust is
> At best a paltry hop
> Around the precincts of the. Bank.   We have
> shut
> The doors and drawn the blinds.
> Our mesmeric visions of an inchoate future
> Glazed by the lure of ' adequate output '
> Lead to a chimerical and chronic blank.

We do not lack our testament and creed,
We have our umbrellas and our A.B.C.'s ;
Morning trousers carry the stripes
Wherewith we are healed in our most need,
And out of bowler hats are conjured
Our decalogue of taste and conduct
Adapted to the exigence of speed.

. . . .

We do not lack money for the Arts ;
A fifty-shilling tailor will have an option
On them, or failing him someone
Who floods the market with cheap motor cars. . . .

The soul has precipices, slippery footholds. Fearful
To stand amid the whorlèd rocks and antres vast
We send our women substitutes to cull
A snippet of ' culture ' in an easy grotto,
Thus content to bow the knee to a garbled past
And propitiate our superstitions by jangling
Votive chords and a bar or two of Chopin.
But perhaps our academic few
Have chosen overmuch to refute
Themselves. Why cannot beauty dwell where it
    pleases,
Unsubject to the oneness or the whatness,
Rhythm of parts, the infant Hercules
Of the categorical mind, strangling
In each hand one attribute ?

. . . .

This,[1] where it is most like Pound, is strongly
characteristic Bottrall, and there is a great deal in
it, especially in the latter part, that is utterly unlike anything that Pound could have done.   What
looks like a reference to Hopkins—

---

[1] *Salute to them that know.*

> (O the mind, mind has mountains ; cliffs of fall
> Frightful . . .)

—may not be one, but the fact that we can be so reminded (this is not to be obtuse to the irony) of one of the ' terrible ' sonnets emphasizes the difference between Mr Bottrall's sensibility and Mr Pound's. (Mr Bottrall, indeed, has learnt something from Hopkins technically.)

In the spirit of his preoccupation with the modern world Mr Bottrall less resembles Mr Pound than Mr Eliot : he is concerned with something more than its uncongeniality to the artist. His world is Mr Eliot's ; a world in which the traditions are bankrupt, the cultures uprooted and withering, and the advance of civilization seems to mean death to distinction of spirit and fineness of living. *The Future is not for us* runs one of his best poems :

> The future is not for us, though we can set up
> Our barriers, rest in our dead-embered
> Sphere, till we come to pause over our last loving-
> cup
> With death.   We are dismembered
> Into a myriad broken shadows,
> Each to himself reflected in a splinter of that glass
> Which we once knew as cosmos, and the close
> Of our long progress is hinted by the crass
> Fogs creeping slow and darkly
> From out the middle west.   We can humanize,
> We can build new temples for the body,
> Set our intellect to tilt against the spies

Of fortune, call this Chance or that Fate,
Estimate the logical worth of ' it may depend . . .',
But we know that we are at the gate
Leading out of the path
Which was to be an Amen having neither beginning
    nor end.

It is a striking proof of Mr Bottrall's originality
that he can so express his sense of the cultural
situation that produced *The Waste Land* without
offering any reminiscence of *The Waste Land* in
rhythm or imagery.   And though he is so sensible
of the disabilities besetting the conscious in this
age, of the inner disintegration responding to the
outer, of the absence of solid ground or fixed
landmarks, yet he differs from the Eliot of *The
Waste Land* in a certain positive energy, an assurance expressing itself at times that there is a course
to steer, that bearings can be found, that there is
a possible readjustment to the conditions.

It is perhaps not extravagant to conjecture that
this difference is representative ; that we have
here the voice of a generation that is, as it were,
becoming acclimatized, or, to change the metaphor, acquiring new habits of equilibrium or
learning to swim.   The positive energy may
be felt in Mr Bottrall's rhythms even when they
express frustration and undirectedness.   And it
comes out explicitly again and again in something
towards which his poetry as a whole is seen to
move.   We have an impressive instance in the

close of a poem already quoted from, *Salute to them that know* :

> There is yet time, even though the clock
> Is set, there is yet time to brave
> The annals of our age, to put our ' wave
> Of progress ' in its proper place, recant
> Our late betrayal and plant
> Within the shadow of the rock
> Our bloodless bodies.   Ask, ask.   Yet
> There is time to break the barricadoes hard
> Hammered against the looked-for synthesis,
> To discard our Chaplin-hero
> In child-lost-like myopic round
> .Beating against the legs of a giant Talus in an iron
>   mask,
> Avoiding hardly the automatic strokes
> Dealt by his flail.
> Time to call up Eros armed to his new Psychean task
> Of mobilizing moving dunes of grainèd sand
> Into an adamantine pyramid
> Rising upward, upward.

We find it again in the magnificent close of *Arion Anadyomenos*, his most ambitious poem before *The Loosening*. The positive assurance is the more impressive here in that it follows upon a passage in which the devastations of excessive consciousness are realized with great personal immediacy.

> ' Is it worth while to make lips smile again,
> To transmit that uneasiness in us which craves
> A moment's mouthing, craves to bully the pain
> The pain and pity of it into staves

Of crabbed pothooks, filling the breadth
Of title-page to colophon?
Is it worth while to debate upon
The automatic sense which forces us
To circumvent our quietus
And put instead on record
Reactions to the vibrations of a vocal chord?'

The waters are lifting at length, and stand revealed
The shoddy roofs steeled,
Even silvered, by reflected light, quite rent
From their cadaverous cerement,
While the final passacaglia of Brahms
Weaves itself point by point
Into the shuddering waves of rain,
Assertive, affirmative, triumphant . . .
Perchance, after all, living within
And for ourselves, exhaling our entity
In our perceptions, yet not altogether bent
With our breaths to petrify and eternize
Some stony replica, we have tracked
What song the sirens sang. So may the disjoint
Time resolve itself and raise up dolphins backed
Like whales to waft us where a confident sea
Is ever breaking, never spent.

The grounds for this positive note are not matter
for debate—at any rate here. The assurance
justifies itself: those rhythms are not to be dealt
with by argument.

A like positive culmination closes, more subtly,
The Loosening, which, as it were, resumes and
comments his poetry up till now. This poem,
which is half-a-dozen or more pages long, is

partly dramatic in presentment, and exhibits great
variety of theme, movement and tone.   The
temptation to consider it in some detail must be
resisted : the immediate point regards its end.
The poet glimpses here a recovered spontaneity,
a readjustment to life, an ability to ride it easily,
analogous to the buoyant, prelapsarian ' naturalness ' of the farm-girl who

> Poised herself like a falcon at check
> Amid the unfooted ploughland,
> Laughter splashing from her mouth and
> Rippling down her brown neck ;
> Not passion-rent she
> But sensing in the bound
> Of her breasts vigours to come, free
> As air and powered to make her one
> With the stream of earth-life around.

Must we despair of attaining a new naturalness at
the far side of the experience of disharmony ?

This much of crude interpretation is ventured
merely to indicate the relation of Mr Bottrall's
poetry to those problems of the modern world
which have intruded themselves again and again
in this book.   It would be more satisfactory to
dwell upon his technique : his power to convince
lies in his rhythms and his imagery.   His rhythms
may be found difficult at first ; but they are subtle,
varied and sure : he uses the body and sinew of
the language.   His imagery is proof that he has
that without which technique is nothing.   The

following, for instance (it is representative), is as
inevitable as it is subtle :

> There were snowdrops on the ground,
> (I met one's sapless frame but now
> Indenting the pages of some book,
> Physiological shall we say ?)

Even when the passage is thus isolated the force
of that 'physiological' tells, and the poignant
concentration of the implicit metaphor is apparent.
As for distinctively modern imagery fused ' experientially ' in the ' emotive furnace,' this illustrates his superb command of it :

> What of the scurry at
> A street-intersection ?   Men lurching forward
> From out the ferro-concrete blocks
> And peering into vacancy ; so many gray and black
> Vultures moving on the scent of carrion in
> A hyperbolic curve, forever nearer
> But forever thwarted.   They never
> Swoop.   No rack for them, even,
> Only the final flutter of a withered
> Leaf towards earth's more potent gravitational field
>   and
> The fibres of its skeleton.

This passage illustrates also how inseparably his
command of imagery is bound up with his
command of rhythm.

A fair account of him would not have been
given without some reference to his suppleness
and complexity of tone and attitude and his wit.

Something of these has appeared in passages already quoted: the variety is too great to exemplify. It is enough to say here that a poem like *Miles Ingloriosus* is a more remarkable achievement than may appear at first sight.

Mr Bottrall's work clinches felicitously the argument of this book, and sanctions high hopes for the future. It would be an unnecessary bathos to turn now to other writers whose work is interesting merely, or mainly, as evidencing that the intelligent young in the direction of their efforts are bearing out the conclusions come to here: the re-orientation has been effected.

But, nevertheless, it is impossible not to revert to a kind of misgiving about the future of poetry touched on in the introductory chapter of this book. Without a public poetry can hardly continue, and the ordinary cultivated reader is ceasing to read poetry at all. The current anthologies are proof enough of this: the complete absence of standards that they reveal implies also the absence of an educated public. As for education, the two anthologies called *Poems of To-day* that (with the endorsement of the English Association) are so widely used in schools hardly contain five good poems between them. There have been bad poets in every age; there is no need to dwell upon the success of Mr Humbert Wolfe. It is more significant that verse-writers should enjoy high reputations—even be admitted to the company of the ' immortals '—whom it is hard to believe that any one can ever have read at any length.

The Testament of Beauty was a best seller, and we shall never know what proportion of the amount of it bought was read. But it is plain that its sales show mainly with what success adroit journalism can exploit even a vestigial habit. Some figures supplied by a firm of publishers specializing in poetry seem relevant at this point. Messrs Sidgwick and Jackson brought out recently a book [1] containing selections from the verse of five writers, and they explain in a *Publishers' Preface* the reason for the experiment : to publish the writers separately would have meant certain heavy loss.

> One of the five MSS. was the 999th of 1000 poetical MSS. (exclusive of those of poets of known standing) received, registered and read by the publishers in the decade which ended 31st December 1929. Of the 1000 MSS. the publishers have accepted and published fifteen, by twelve authors. Two of the fifteen volumes have paid their way. The twelve authors have shared £73, 4s. 4d. The publishers have lost, on the fifteen books, a little more than double that sum.

It does indeed look (the quality of the verse chosen emphasizes the conclusion) as if respect for poetry were mainly a vestigial habit. All

[1] *A Faggot of Verse*, 1930.

traces of it, almost, have disappeared in the vast masses catered for by the popular press. Of all verse-writers with any claim to literary standing, the present Laureate probably comes nearest to popularity. Yet, when he was crowned, the event had no news-value for the popular Sunday papers published immediately afterwards.

The ordinary cultivated reader is ceasing to be able to read poetry. In self-defence amid the perpetual avalanche of print he has had to acquire reading habits that incapacitate him when the signals for unaccustomed and subtle responses present themselves.[1] He has, moreover, lost the education that in the past was provided by tradition and social environment. Even the poetry of simple sensibility, if it is not superficially familiar, seems incomprehensible to him. And the more important poetry of the future is unlikely to be simple.

For not only poetry, but literature and art in general, are becoming more specialized : the process is implicit in the process of modern civilization. The important works of to-day, unlike those of the past, tend to appeal only at the highest level of response, which only a tiny minority can reach, instead of at a number of levels. On the other hand, the finer values are

---

[1] Mr I. A. Richards in *Practical Criticism* offers some striking evidence on this matter.

ceasing to be a matter of even conventional concern for any except the minority capable of the highest level. Everywhere below, a process of standardization, mass-production and levelling-down goes forward, and civilization is coming to mean a solidarity achieved by the exploitation of the most readily released responses. So that poetry in the future, if there is poetry, seems likely to matter even less to the world.[1]

Those who care about it can only go on caring.

[1] The present writer has produced a good deal of representative data relevant to this paragraph in *Mass Civilization and Minority Culture*.

Retrospect 1950

IT is now nearly twenty years since this book was written. I do not, however, propose anything in the nature of 'bringing it up to date'. It was written as an attempt to define the situation in English poetry at that given moment; a moment when the accomplishment of what amounted to a revolution, the upshot of the most significant work of the previous decade or two, needed to be critically recognised. I aimed at showing in what new ways the present of English poetry must now be seen as related to the past. That 'present' has itself receded into the past; but such *raison d'être* as the book can boast is bound up with the originating purpose and the closeness with which the the book pursues it. And I may relevantly add that the re-orientation described in it is to-day very generally recognized as a historical fact, and a critically important one: an account of it that was written in ignorance of subsequent developments may for that reason have a certain interest.

Perhaps I may add, too, that the book itself has some claim to be, in a modest way, a historical fact—written in the given circumstances and with the given aim, it played a certain part in literary history. That is a claim which a very little research will verify—a consideration, however, that would not, alone, have struck me as justifying the risk of appearing egotistical. But there is stronger reason for taking the risk. The history of changes of

taste and acceptance—how they come about—
may have more than an academic interest; not only
are there morals to draw that have practical bearings, but contemplation of the process of change
may make us more fully aware of what has happened, what the new enlightenment really is, and
how much or how little it favours life.

The particular piece of history in question illustrates how, when resistance to the new thing
collapses, the readjustment is effected, orthodoxy
reconsolidated, and the world made safe again.
History will go on repeating itself, so there is
always point in insisting on the moral as represented by the most striking recent instance. But
for recording my note on the development of a
literary-critical orthodoxy there is more to be said:
such an orthodoxy naturally tends to discourage
true respect for the genius it offers to exalt—to
substitute, that is, deference. True respect is inseparable from the concern to see the object as in
itself it really is, to insist on the necessary dis-
criminations, and so to make the essential achievement, with the special life and virtue it embodies,
effective as influence. The new conventional acceptance tends quite otherwise.

Let me start by quoting the one reference to
my own work in Mr F. O. Matthiessen's *The
Achievement of T. S. Eliot* (p. 46):

'F. R. Leavis, *New Bearings in English Poetry* (London,
1932) uses a similar phrase [to one in Mr Matthiessen's
text] on p. 94. Mr Leavis' interpretation of Eliot, though
acutely perceptive of certain details to which I have been
indebted particularly in this chapter, suffers from a

certain over-intensity. He seems to be writing continually on the defensive as though he were the apostle of modern art to an unappreciative world. As a result his criticism, though eager, is somewhat wanting in balance and perspective.'

Already in 1935 (the date of the first edition of his book) Mr Matthiessen is suggesting that the critic who supposed himself to be undertaking anything formidable in trying to get attention for the approach and the valuations defined in *New Bearings in English Poetry* was suffering from illusions. The world, Mr Matthiessen implies, was always ready enough to be 'appreciative'. It may be, of course, that conditions in America were very different from those I knew from experience in England. But I think it reasonable to suggest that the difference in date between his book (1935) and mine (1932) has some bearing on his attitude. The pioneering was done: his work was the easier in more than one respect. One of them will be apparent to anyone who compares his book with mine (which he does indeed commend as helpful in certain details): to clarify the perception, arrive at the judgment, see the significance and define the approach in the first place may be more difficult than Mr Matthiessen supposes, and call for a tension that strikes him as over-intensity.

Then, for another respect, there is this to be noted: when, in spite of the indignant resistance of the academic and literary worlds, the unavoidable recognition of change has become imminent, the critic who by studiously clear and challenging formulation sets himself to precipitate the recognition, and make it as complete and clear as possible, must expect to earn lasting disapproval (he is narrow, his tone is wrong, he is over-intense, he is offensive); but the academic consolidator who follows need fear no animus at all.

In any case, I have to record as a fact of history that the academic world in England, a very few years before Mr Matthiessen's book came out, did, in such views and valuations as he thinks I might have assumed to be generally acceptable, find matter for indignant and punitive opposition. Perhaps I may quote here the testimony I was moved to bear by a passage in the volume of essays on T. S. Eliot that came out recently under the editorship of Dr B. Rajan. The passage runs:

> 'When *The Sacred Wood* and *Homage to John Dryden* appeared Mr Eliot was still the subject of frightened abuse in the weeklies, and also in some academic circles. But his views percolated downwards, and are now almost common form. How was it done'?

And here is the testimony it drew from me; it is very relevant to Mr Matthiessen's suggestion:

'That "still" must appear very odd to anyone who recalls the chronology of Mr Eliot's *œuvre*. *The Sacred Wood* came out in 1920 and *Homage to John Dryden* in 1924 (when in most academic circles Mr Eliot's name would hardly have met with recognition). "Still", I must testify, having the strongest of grounds for confident insistence, still in 1930 (and later), and in the academic circles that now receive Dr Rajan's enterprise without a flutter, Mr Eliot's mere name, however modestly

mentioned, was as a red rag to a bull. I could tell
Miss . . . . . privately, some piquant and true
anecdotes in illustration. I will confine myself here
to two reminiscences of sufficiently public fact.
When in 1929 an innocent young editor printed
an article of mine on Mr Eliot's criticism in *The
Cambridge Review* (a reply to a contemptuous dismissal of him by a Cambridge "English" don in
Mr Desmond McCarthy's *Life and Letters*) he very
soon had cause to realize that he had committed
a scandalous impropriety, and I myself was left in
no doubt as to the unforgivableness of my offence.
And when, in 1932, a book of mine came out that
made a study of Mr Eliot the centre of an attempt
to define the distinctive aspects of significant contemporary poetry, so much worse than imprudent
was it found to be that the advanced academic
intellectual of the day declined (or so the gloating
whisper ran) to have anything to do with it, and
The Cambridge Review could find no reviewer for it
in Cambridge. I remember, too, with some amuse-
ment, the embarrassed notes I received from
correct friends who felt that some form of con-
gratulation on the appearance of a book had to be
gone through, but knew also that the offence was
rank, disastrous and unpardonable. Yet the matter
of that offensive book is seen, in Dr Rajan's sympo-
sium, to be now common form. How was it done?'

Again, I have to record as a verifiable fact of
history that, whatever its faults, and though it
continued to be regarded with the strongest disfavour by those who in the academic and literary

worlds determine where credit is to be given and what books should sell, my book (as comparison readily establishes) was found highly useful by a number of later writers on T. S. Eliot and modern poetry. From before the date of Mr Matthiessen's book onwards to yesterday, a whole series of books has appeared evincing a heavy indebtedness to mine—one of them (this one roundly abusive) enjoyed for a while a great notoriety for it. I will not enumerate the list: anyone who is at all familiar with modern critical literature can provide one.

In stressing this curious history of influence and associated disfavour I am not bent on insinuating any absurd and extravagant claims. On the one hand, I am well aware of what I myself owe to other critics; on the other, I am not in the least inclined to suppose that Mr Eliot's arrival, his genius being what it is, depended on the work of any one advocate. My aim is to throw light on recent literary history. And at the same time it regards the present—the appreciation of certain characteristics of the prevailing state of affairs.

Mr Eliot has become a public institution, a part of the establishment. Nothing brings this home more forcibly or reveals more clearly the conventional nature of his acceptance, than the way in which his later utterances on Milton have been acclaimed and used. The British Academy address was hailed as a critical recantation, in which Mr Eliot confessed himself to have been grievously wrong about Milton in his younger and less discerning days. Milton—that is the feeling—has been vindicated against criticism erroneously supposed to have damaged that massive central part of the establishment, and the great modern poet who has done the service (the worst offences having been committed, not by himself, but by presumptuous, and now obviously ridiculous, followers) has thereby confirmed his own institutional status. What Mr Eliot, in that address, actually says about Milton I have analysed at length elsewhere.[1] But in any case, to put the orthodox value on it is to expose an inappreciation of his most vital criticism, to miss its force, and to deny the essence of that poetic achievement with which the criticism is so closely bound up. For poetry is made of words and rhythms, and 'sensibility alters from generation to generation in everyone . . . but expression is only altered by a man of genius'. It was the informing presence, everywhere in the criticism, of the practitioner's preoccupation with his problem of putting words together—of inventing the ways of using words, the rhythms and the versification—that, in his best days as a critic, gave his brief asides on Milton their potency. Milton remains, of course, a great power in English poetic history, and an intrinsically impressive figure (in spite of some of his defenders), but those who cannot see what is meant by saying that he was a prepotent influence in taste and poetic practice until Mr Eliot's work had its effect, and has since ceased to be, cannot, whatever

[1] 'Mr Eliot and Milton', *The Sewanee Review*, Winter, 1949. To be reprinted in *The Common Pursuit*.

they may suppose, appreciate Mr Eliot's genius
or its achievement. They deny while acclaiming.

That is the essence of the orthodoxy. And the
literary-critical orthodoxy, it has to be noted, is
intimately associated with orthodoxy in religion
—as is observable in the offer to assimilate away
(if I may so put it) his pre-Anglo-Catholic past.
'It is possible to see all his poetry as a single poem'
—that is the current formula. 'The *Four Quartets*
are as necessary to an understanding of *The Waste
Land* as *The Waste Land* is necessary to prepare for
the *Quartets*.' This representative commentator[1]
brings out clearly the part of religious orthodoxy
in the attribution of critical significance to the
later utterances on Milton (concerning whom the
most recent insight, it will be seen, makes it unnecessary to talk of recantation):

> 'His advances have always been bold yet carefully pre-
> pared. And although neither the plan nor the direction
> of the next attack have ever been completely divulged,
> loyalty among his followers has been on the whole un-
> shaken. If he has been consistent, he has also been quite
> incalculable. *The Waste Land* was acclaimed in the
> 'twenties as the great poem of unbelief. It was followed
> by Mr Eliot's confession that he was an Anglo-Catholic
> in religion, a Limited Monarchist in politics, and a
> Classicist in art. Similarly, it was taken for granted
> throughout the 'thirties that Milton should be included
> among the demolitions. In the 'forties the same Milton
> must be taken as among the rehabilitations. And in all
> this there has been no hint of the vacillating, nor any
> sign of a recantation.'

The essence, I said, of the orthodoxy, literary-
critical or religious or both, is to deny the genius

[1] See *The Cambridge Journal*, September 1949.

while acclaiming it; a truth exemplified with peculiar irony in the cult of the *Four Quartets*. There has been a significant tendency in the literary-academic world—and not only in respect of Eliot—to substitute exegesis for criticism: the essential hazard having been taken and the first-hand work of criticism done, the expositor can assume the essential judgments and let his expositions of structure, themes, and significances show his adequacy to the rare and difficult masterpiece. The tendency of the expositor to misrepresent, and, in effect, to deny, the genius of his author is peculiarly apparent in the fashionable elucidations of *Four Quartets*. The approach is made from the point of view of doctrinal acceptance: the expositor, bringing up his theology and his studiously acquired knowledge of Mr Eliot's own reading, and knowing beforehand (he feels) what in a general way the poetry is about and what it means, reduces it to a poetic presentment of familiar doctrines. The grateful reader, with a sense of having grasped the 'meaning', takes away the familiar general formulations instead of the poetry, the exegesis having abetted the common propensity to arrive without having travelled. Thus is frustrated the enormous labour expended by the poet in undercutting mere acceptance, inhibiting mere acquiescence, and circumventing, at every level, what may be called cliché.

For Mr Eliot is a much greater and more significant poet than his Anglo-Catholic admirers make him. He is also more disturbing. His religious

poetry, read for what it is, disturbs radically, by
the depth and subtlety of its analysis: it explores
the nature of believing, and the nature of conceptual thought; in relation, especially, to religious
dogma. Its extreme continence (defeating the
'lethargy of habit') in the use of the conceptual
currency goes with an extreme continence of
affirmation. I have discussed it under these aspects
elsewhere.[1] Here I will only say that it comes
from the mind that could once write in prose[2]—
though in the habit since of saving its finer vigour
and courage for poetry:

> 'I cannot see that poetry can ever be separated from
> something which I should call belief, and to which I
> cannot see any reason for refusing the name of belief,
> unless we are to shuffle names altogether. It should
> hardly be needful to say that it will not inevitably be
> orthodox Christian belief, although that possibility can
> be entertained, since Christianity will probably continue
> to modify itself into *something* that can be believed in (I
> do not mean *conscious* modifications like modernism,
> etc., which always have the opposite effect). The major-
> ity of people live below the level of belief or doubt.
> It takes application and a kind of genius to believe any-
> thing, and to believe anything (I do *not* mean merely
> to believe in some "religion") will probably become
> more and more difficult as time goes on.'

Eliot's genius is that of the great poet who has
a profound and acute apprehension of the difficulties of his age. One doesn't need to be able to
share Mr Eliot's personal Anglo-Catholicism, or
even be able to sympathize with it, or anything

[1] *Education and the University*, Appendix I.
[2] In Wyndham Lewis's *The Enemy*, January 1927.

akin to it, in order to feel indebted to *Four Quartets*, and to see that this poetry has the most important relevance to the interests of anyone fully alive in our time.

*　　*　　*

I said above, in explaining why I had dismissed the idea of bringing this book 'up to date', that an account of the great re-orientation described in it which was written in ignorance of subsequent developments might for that reason have a certain value. I have now to confess that subsequent developments, as I see them, have not been of such a kind as I should care to write about at length. And here, I suppose, I ought to admit a score against myself; for in speaking of the 're-orientation' as having made possible a modern English poetry I might reasonably have been supposed to entertain—as I did—not unhopeful expectations. Actually, I think the history of English poetry since then has been depressing in the extreme.

Mr Eliot, of course, has continued his creative career, hardly paralleled in its successive renewals; and the presence of so great a poet, producing and still developing, has given the period life and distinction. But if he had stopped writing after *Ash-Wednesday*, what would that period have had to show? The answer to that question is what I find depressing. Some four or five years ago, on the reopening of relations between this country and France, I was asked by the visiting *conseil de rédaction* of a French review what, looking back, I could report as having happened in English poetry during the previous ten years. The question was a disconcerting one. The circumstances didn't favour an evasive elaboration of comment on *Four Quartets*. All I could find to say was: 'Yeats has died, and Eliot has gone on'. And that seems to me an epitome of the years that have passed since I took my note of the 'new bearings', and reported the signs of promise. (Mr Eliot had made other poets possible—that was certainly my theme). So, in spite of Mr Eliot's own magnificent performance, the sanguineness of the now remote critic, reviewed across the record of the intervening years, looks to me, I confess, if pardonable, a little pathetic.

Of course, already in those opening 'thirties a Poetic Renaissance was supposed to have opened too. A number of names were current as those of promising, and even established, young poets. One reason why my book, though widely used among publicists of Modern Poetry, itself received little favour or, even, mention, was that it neither acclaimed the Renaissance nor mentioned the names, the owners of which were to exercise a predominant influence in the literary world for years to come. I naturally knew of the Renaissance and had heard of the names; but I judged that it was early yet for acclamation.

In fact, only one of these new reputations appeared to me to be supported by gifts of any promise, and that was W. H. Auden's. I did not discuss him in my book, because the promise, as I saw it, could not be asserted without a weight of qualifying and privative emphasis that, in the absence of anything to be acclaimed as *done*, might, I feared, make the introduction for such treatment seem wantonly offensive. It was the 'Charade', *Paid on Both Sides*, published in *The Criterion* in 1929, that first called attention to Auden. This curious and youthful piece might have represented the very green immaturity of a notable creative talent. But the author, it was plain, would have to work very hard, resist temptations, and achieve through discipline and maturing experience a difficult development, before anything satisfactory could come of his gifts. The childlike vividness of imagination was accompanied by the disabilities of the childish; the verbal vigour went with an obscurity of the wrong kind—that which betrays incoherence and lack of meaning; and, peculiarly ominous because of the attendant sophistication, there was, manifest in the writer's uncertainty as to the degree of seriousness he intended, a surprising radical adolescence that should have been already well outgrown. It seems to me that Auden has hardly come nearer to essential maturity since, though he made a rapid advance in sophistication.[1]

[1] I may say that this placing of Auden has been enforced in *Scrutiny* by detailed criticism in more than half a dozen reviews, coming from half a dozen different hands. The dismissal of Spender (once in conventional esteem the Shelley of the Poetic Renaissance), Day Lewis, MacNeice, George Barker, Dylan Thomas, has also been done critically in *Scrutiny*. My brief placing reference to Empson and Bottrall has also its due backing there in a number of reviews by different hands.

Sophistication—that is a topic which presents itself again when we contemplate the failure to develop, or to develop satisfactorily, of the two young poets I do mention in my book, Empson and Bottrall. The diagnosis of sophistication is relevant to a great deal of the characteristic work of the early nineteen-thirties. There is that impressiveness of modish cultural equipment; that air of knowing one's way about; in short, that preoccupation with intellectuality, and the externals of profundity and subtlety; and, underneath, the correlated failure in personal development: nothing seems to happen at that depth, the established aim and bent hardly permitting it to happen. Sophistication belongs to a climate in which the natural appetite for kudos is not chastened by contact with mature standards, and in which fixed immaturity can take itself for something else.

Such a climate prevailed in the world in which Auden made his *début*—Auden whose career is worth pondering because it is the representative career of the nineteen-thirties, and has a representative significance. He entered the literary world with a reputation made at the university: as a recent critic in *The Times Literary Supplement* puts it, he was 'the Oxford intellectual with a bag of poetic squibs in his pocket'. What this critic doesn't say, or appear to realize, is that the Auden who conquered the literary world with such ease was the undergraduate intellectual. The undergraduate coterie has always had its part in the formation of talent; but the coterie in the ancient seats of learning has tended, in other days, to bring its members into touch with adult standards. That which formed Auden seems to have been able to remain utterly unaware of them. And, what was worse for him, he cannot have noticed any essential differences when he passed from undergraduate Oxford into the world where the canon of contemporary literature is established, and the currency of accepted valuations stamped. The Oxford valuation became immediately metropolitan. The undergraduate notability became a world-figure almost overnight. Auden was accepted as, beyond question, a leading intellectual and a major poet. His admirers spoke of him as having superseded T. S. Eliot.

It was ridiculous; but not, for that, the less disastrous. Greater gifts than Auden's might have lost, in such a success, their chance of coming to anything. His misfortune, in fact, brings vividly before us the conditions that, in our time, work against the maturation and development of any young talent. They may be seen, simply, as the failure of the function of criticism, though that, of course, is only one aspect of a very large and complex fact. This may be seen, again, as the disintegration of the educated reading public. It is only in such a public that critical standards have their effective existence. Where there *is* one, the critic, even when advancing judgments that challenge the most generally accepted valuations, may hope, if he expresses his judgments cogently and aims them with sufficient address at the critical conscience, to get the weight of corroborative response with him, and so to tell. But where no such public exists to be appealed to, the critic's unpopular judgments, even if he can get them printed, remain mere arbitrary assertions and offensive attitudes.

These are truisms, but they are truisms that, for one engaged in such a retrospect as the present, have a lively relevance. And here are two others: a coterie naturally protects itself and its members, as far as it can, from the severities of criticism: where the whole literary world, so far as current critical expression is concerned, falls virtually under the control of something in the nature of a coterie, then the conditions for the development of creative talent are very bad indeed.

The failure of the function of criticism, the disintegration of the educated reading public: there is no need to do more by way of explaining these phrases than refer to the process that one tends to represent by the name of Lord North- cliffe. The war of 1914 greatly accelerated the adverse consequences of the process. Those in a position to make the comparison will agree, I think, that things were very decidedly worse in 1930 than in 1920. I know that what is involved is a whole massive and complex movement of civilization, but my concern here is with the function of criticism. I think there is some point in such a concern—I say this in a practical rather than a theoretical spirit. For every man has his own job, and however discouraging a report an

inclusive survey of the drift of things may leave
him with, there is always what may be called a
middle-range end that he should be able to propose for himself as worth his work and his hope.
And, granted the disintegration of the educated
public, it doesn't follow that one must assume the
futility of all effort to assert the function of
criticism. On the contrary, the fragments still represent the potentiality of a public that, the right
means being taken, might be brought into
effective life—a public small by the measures of
mass-civilization, but not therefore negligible.
(Even in a mass-civilization, size is not everything.)

In fact, if a public that cannot make its existence
felt, can, without too great a paradox, be said to
be one, then the educated public that is necessary
to the maintenance of the critical function has
continued to exist (one assumes that, in assuming
the cause not lost); the problem is to circumvent
and defeat the conditions of a mass-civilization
world that deprive it of organs of expression,
cohesion and effect, and so make it no better than
non-existent.

These were the convictions of the group that,
in the early 'thirties, founded *Scrutiny*, a quarterly
that was to have its base in an ancient university,
and, by way of vindicating the Idea of a University, to perform the function of a metropolitan
review (though it didn't—and doesn't—pay con-
tributors and staff). We knew, of course, that a
due activity of the function of criticism would

mean collaboration with other centres—the collaboration of critical exchange and interplay. We didn't find it possible to count much, for these, on the well-known and influential weekly that was to go on increasing its circulation so portentously through the decade. But *The Criterion*— that there was practical relevance in the existence of that organ it didn't occur to us to doubt. We assumed a corresponding view to ours of the critical function, and of the urgent need. We were wrong.

. The young writers of the Poetic Renaissance (it is poetry I am concerned with in this retrospect) were emphatically Left-inclined—Marxist and Marxising. The quarterly in question had an official bent towards Anglo-Catholicism, and was editorially associated with political attitudes suggestive of the influence of Charles Maurras. But the young poetical Communists and fellow-travellers and their friends were able to make themselves as much at home in its review-pages as in *The New Statesman and Nation*. For their purposes it became, incongruously, their organ, and their purposes did not include—did not permit—the revival of the function of criticism. A brief reconnaissance of the bound volumes will reveal the truth, and the moderation, of this account. And in this way—it is an ironical fact— was ensured, not only the immunity of these young writers from any disturbing critical challenge, but that general abeyance of the function which sufficiently explains why the influence of

T. S. Eliot, out of which a poetic revival seemed so likely to come, should have been so sadly defeated.

It is not in terms of the triumph of any coterie that one would describe the essence of the situation to-day. The lapsed function has slipped out of memory, and the literary world that makes the reputations gleaned by dons, dons' wives, university-educated school teachers, and the educated classes in general; from the review pages of the Sunday papers can follow its natural promptings without embarrassment. It is natural, and not necessarily unamiable, to like kudos, and to see the point of pleasing a friend. The lengths to which the process of turning the social values into the distinctions and glories of contemporary literature can be carried (the context, I think, makes the force of 'social' plain) has been strikingly demonstrated in the recent elevation of a whole family to the status of living classics.

It is significant that New York should have added its homage so readily and so unanimously. The system, in fact, is international. At home, it makes the ancient universities, or the relevant elements in them, a part of the literary world. As for the B.B.C., it must be enough to say that the Third Programme on the literary side is a very different thing from the Third Programme in music. And if my account of the tendency and inclusiveness of the system should seem to anyone exaggerated, I recommend a study of two booklets published for the British Council: *Poetry since 1939* by Mr Stephen Spender, and *Prose Literature since 1939* by Mr John Hayward.

A friend of mine who holds a Chair of English on the Continent complained to me not long ago that he found it impossible to question with any effect what may be called the *Horizon* valuations of contemporary English writers. 'People—students of English—ask me what I think of Stephen Spender, Dylan Thomas, Edith Sitwell, and when I say, I'm being indecent; I'm fouling my own nest! They *know*. They know the facts, and these reputations are basic *données*; they're as unquestionable literary facts as any they know. Who are the cultural emissaries and *liaison* officers?—Need I say? They meet their equivalents in the European capitals. It's a European system.'—To which I added, producing a copy of *Partisan Review* for December 1948, that it looked like embracing America also.

Here, then, is the report that I have to make when asked what has happened in English poetry since this book was written. It is a depressing report, and convicts me of having been oversanguine at the time of the Poetic Renaissance which (nevertheless) I refused to acclaim. I am not, of course, saying that verse-writers of some interest have not appeared. But what I have said conveys, I sadly believe, the essential truth. To propose for oneself the indelicate duty of saying it may perhaps seem pointlessly officious and temerarious, for if it *is* the truth, what chance has its utterance of producing any useful effect? Yet a critic must believe, while he believes in anything, that there is point in trying to call attention to the disastrousness of letting the function of criticism be forgotten. And perhaps the very extravagance of recent triumphs of what I have for convenience called the 'social values', in what should be the field of literary criticism, makes the present moment a better one than there has been for some time for my observations on the system that, in its workings and its tendencies, those astonishing triumphs exemplify.

If the hopes, then, of twenty years ago have proved ill-founded, both the major valuations, and the general case, presented in *New Bearings in English Poetry*, have stood; in fact, they have come to look like recognitions of the obvious. It is odd now to recall the indignation with which the book was received.

Of the major figures dealt with in the book, Pound, though he has written much since (and is still writing), is the one of whom my general sense has been least modified. Of *Hugh Selwyn Mauberley* I think as highly as ever: it seems to me a great poem, and a weightier achievement than any single thing—for *Mauberley* does form a whole—to be found in Yeats. As for the *Cantos*, there are more of them than there were when I first wrote about Pound, and the more of them there are, the plainer does it become that they tend to obscure rather than to strengthen Pound's real claims. I am not at all impressed when I am told by enthusiasts that I ought in consistency to admire them, since they merely employ on a larger scale the methods of Mauberley.

I think that Mr Eliot did Pound and criticism an ill service when he threw out that tip about the superiority of the *Cantos* and their great technical value; a value he defined for himself by saying that he was not interested in what Pound had to say, but only in his way of saying it. To-day it is assumed that if one withholds one's admiration from the *Pisan Cantos*, it must be because one's dislike of the Fascism and Anti-Semitism in what Pound says (and my own dislike is intense) prevents one from recognizing the beauty and genius of the saying. But how boring that famous versification actually is—boring with the emptiness of the egotism it thrusts on us. A poet's creativity can hardly be a matter of mere versification; there is no profound creative impulse at all for Pound's technical skill to serve. He has no real creative theme. His versification and his *procédés* are servants of wilful ideas and platform vehemences. His moral attitudes and absolutisms are bullying assertions, and have the uncreative blatancy of one whose Social Credit consorts naturally with Fascism and Anti-Semitism. It still remains true that only in *Mauberley* has he achieved the impersonality, substance, and depth of great poetry. The classical status of *Mauberley*, however, hasn't anything like general recognition—a fact that throws a depressing light on the supposed liveliness of current interest in contemporary verse.

Of Hopkins I am perhaps more aware of the limitations than I was when I wrote my chapter on him. Not that it doesn't seem to me to stand well enough, and I think it was not ill-designed for its purpose. When I wrote it, I aimed, not at a definitive placing of Hopkins, but at establishing his existence as a challenging fact, of great significance for any critical view of the immediate past of English poetry. It may be already forgotten that, so short a while back, Hopkins needed that kind of championship. Actually, I can testify that well on into the 'thirties, Professors of Poetry and of English Literature, confident in the support of those whose opinion mattered to them, were voicing freely their scorn for anyone who could take Hopkins seriously.

The change of attitude occurred almost overnight. Hopkins, it suddenly appeared, was a classic, a glory of the establishment, worth the most arduous researches and the minutest annotations of scholarship. This was in the middle 'thirties. The industry throve, and by now there is a large Hopkins literature. The Letters, especially those to Bridges, are something to be grateful for. But the scholarly studies, for the most part, can serve little function but that of helping lecturers and examination candidates to be plausibly irrelevant.

Hopkins, it is true, did himself take an interest in Greek metres and Welsh poetic; but, nevertheless, there is no need to study his 'debt' to the Greek and the Welsh in order to understand his own art. If one cannot, out of one's knowledge of the English language as used in living speech and by Shakespeare, understand the spirit of Hopkins' anti-Tennysonian art and respond to his compressions and licenses (even if there is further to be recognized the special bent towards 'inscape'), then it will hardly be understanding that one is helped to by these erudite researches.

It seems to me that my chapter on him does sufficiently do what it set out to do: indicate the approach from which the impressive fact of Hopkins becomes undeniable. I have already admitted (in a centenary essay on him[1]) that, powerful as his genius was, I should now feel bound to stress the limitations. *For early did he leave the world:* the stuff of experience he commanded for poetry was extremely limited, and it is plain that the intensity of 'doing' that marked his art, with its overmastering bent for pattern, is to be correlated with this fact. There is some justice in Mr Eliot's description of him (see *After Strange Gods*, p. 48) as a 'nature poet'—though it still seems to me deplorable that Mr Eliot should at the same time have seen fit to bracket him with Meredith.

[1] *Scrutiny*, Vol. XII, No. 2. To be reprinted in *The Common Pursuit*.